Stop Growing Broke

START
GROWING
PROFIT$

Stop Growing Broke

START
GROWING
PROFIT$

Systems, Sanity, and the
Secret to Real Profitability

KAREN HAIRSTON

CERTIFIED

(H)

WRITTEN
BY HUMAN

DEDICATION

To Pete, Kristen, Erich, and Carter—

Thank you for your love, patience, and all the takeout meals that fueled this book.

Kristen, special shout-out for pushing me to think outside the box—especially when it came to the cover.

I'm so grateful for a family that cheered me on, even when it meant hearing, "We're having that for dinner again?" more than once. 😊

CONTENTS

From Growing Broke to Growing Profits

Your sales are up with no profit growth,
Why can't the direction be up for both?
The chaos creeps in more each day,
And you can't figure out another way.

You've hired fast, you've bought new tools,
You've followed frameworks—and presumably golden rules.
You've done the work to spark a change—
But things still feel just out of range.

But what if scale meant something more—
Not just more work, but something sure?
A business built to run with grace,
That thrives without you in the place.

So here's the shift: lead systems-first.
Fix the leaks before the pipes burst.
Go for freedom, flow, and steady gains—
With a stronger frame that still remains.

Decide. Document. Dry Run. Define.
Deploy the system—make it shine.
Then test and tweak the way you grow—
Progress speeds up by taking it slow.

Now clarity becomes your guide.
Your team steps up. You step aside.
You're scaling now and all's aligned—
You've stopped growing broke—and grow profits by design.

INTRODUCTION

From Growing Broke to Growing Profits

---

*"Making money is not the same as making
a business work."*
— Michael E. Gerber

The Day That Never Ends

Alex scans 72 new emails. Her project manager is already at her door—and it's not even 8 a.m.

Their best developer just resigned. A major client is threatening to pull out.

By lunchtime, she hasn't touched her inbox.

By 6:00 p.m., she's racing to her son's hockey game—still answering Slack messages from the parking lot. And at midnight, she's at the kitchen table with her laptop open, trying to make sense of financials that don't add up. Sales are up. Expenses are up. But the bank account? Not so much.

The business is technically growing, but it doesn't feel like progress.

Alex started this company for more freedom—more control over her time, her money, and her life.

Now, she's constantly putting out fires, juggling too much, and wondering why more revenue hasn't made anything easier.

Sound familiar?

Maybe your numbers are up, but you're still not sleeping well. Maybe your team is good, but you're still the glue holding everything together. Maybe you've hit a revenue milestone that should feel exciting... but all you can think about is how to cover next quarter.

If you're running a small but growing business, you've probably had your own "Alex" days—when your team is stretched thin, your inbox is stacked. You're holding the business together with sheer determination, when one more resignation—or one more missed invoice—might push you over the edge.

You're doing everything you can to hold it all together—and it still doesn't feel like enough.

You're not the only one.

And the problem isn't you—it's what your business is missing behind the scenes.

More Revenue, More Problems?

If your revenue is increasing but your profits are decreasing, you're not alone. In fact, it's more common than you think—and it's exactly why I wrote this book.

Too many CEOs and business owners hit a point where things get harder—not easier—even as the business grows. It's not because you've made a critical mistake. It's not because you haven't worked hard enough.

It's because most businesses aren't built to grow profitably, at least at first. Systems, financial structures, and team operations often evolve reactively, duct-taped together on the fly, without a solid foundation underneath.

As a result, growth—especially rapid growth—just exposes the gaps that were already there.

You see it in the missed invoices, the late payments, the expenses that climb faster than you expected. You land a big contract—but you still get a knot in your stomach when you run payroll. Revenue is up, but somehow you still can't pay yourself reliably.

You start hiring to keep up with demand, but the onboarding is rushed—or worse, nonexistent. Quality slips. Clients get frustrated. You feel like you're running harder just to stay in place.

Then someone suggests a new tool or software—again. But layering more on top of a fragile foundation doesn't solve the real problem. It just adds more chaos and increases the risk of collapse. Most fixes treat the symptoms, not the root cause.

What's happening here has a name: **you're growing broke.**

When the Numbers Don't Add Up

Growing broke means your business is bringing in more revenue, but profitability is heading in the opposite direction. You're growing without the systems and financial clarity needed to ensure those extra dollars lead to stronger margins and healthier cash flow, which means you're not scaling sustainably.

You don't set out to grow broke—it happens quietly. A few extra expenses that never quite get reconciled. A big new client who takes more resources than expected. A key hire who's still not fully ramped up. You look at the profit and loss statement and wonder why it doesn't reflect how busy everyone's been.

And because no one taught you how to read financial reports for patterns—only totals—you miss the early signs. Profit is down, but sales are up—so it must be timing, right? Maybe a billing delay? Or a one-time thing?

But cash flow issues are often systems problems in disguise. The numbers might look like a financial glitch, but they're often signaling deeper operational gaps—and then that "one-time thing" happens again. And again.

Eventually, you realize: this isn't a blip. It's a pattern. The numbers are trying to tell you something.

The solution isn't to work harder. It's to build a business that's structurally sound—financially, operationally, and culturally.

Growth isn't the enemy. But growth without structure? That's when things start to unravel.

What It's Costing You to Stay Stuck

If you don't fix the foundation, the problems won't magically disappear. Instead, the cracks just widen.

- You land new clients—but can't figure out where the profit went.
- Your team burns out—or bails—because the pace is unsustainable.
- You stop looking at the numbers because they make your stomach churn.
- You wonder how much longer you can keep pushing before something breaks.

The real cost isn't just financial. It's in the time spent re-explaining tasks that should already be documented. In the team meetings where problems surface but are never solved. In the lost sleep, wondering if your clients are as happy as they say. In the pressure to maintain the appearance of growth, even when you're secretly feeling stretched thin.

And underneath it all, you start to question whether the way you're running the business is really working—whether it will ever give back what you've put in.

You didn't start this to build a high-stress job you can't escape. At some point, something has to change. If you keep doing what you're doing, you'll keep getting what you've got.

But what's the best way to start doing things differently?

By starting with the right foundation.

What Starts to Work for Real

Once you stop reacting to symptoms and start fixing the structure, everything changes.

You get a clearer picture of what's working—and what's costing you more than it's worth. Clarity is the first lever of control. It helps you shift from reaction mode to intentional action. You no longer have to hold every detail in your head or answer every question yourself. Your systems work. Your people step up. Your numbers finally make sense.

The results?

- Healthier, more predictable profit margins
- A team that runs without constant oversight
- Projects delivered with consistency—and less chaos
- Greater confidence in your financial decisions
- Stronger control over your time

You can finally take a real vacation without checking email every hour. You stop saying, "I'll just do it myself"—because you don't have to anymore. Your bookkeeper sends reports you can actually understand. And you start making decisions based on data—not just gut feel and crossed fingers.

That's what becomes possible when you build a business designed to scale from the inside out.

Clarity Made the Difference

Devon runs operations for a small virtual reality company. The team was talented and committed, but projects kept stalling, and no one could pinpoint why. Deadlines slipped. Cash flow felt unpredictable. And Devon was constantly in reaction mode.

So they paused and mapped out one core delivery process—just one. They documented the steps, clarified who owned what, and added a 15-minute weekly check-in to stay aligned. Within a month, misunderstandings dropped, turnaround time improved, and financial reports finally started to reflect reality.

Devon didn't overhaul the whole business. They simply stopped guessing—and started making decisions with clarity.

These are the results of doing the right things in the right order: starting small, building strong, and adapting as you go.

Building smart systems and making data-driven decisions isn't about abandoning your values or trading your soul for a spreadsheet. It's about making sure the business you've built actually supports the life you want.

Because structure doesn't limit freedom, it creates it. That's when clarity becomes currency.

Start Simple, Build Strong

You don't need another productivity hack—or to cram 14 hours of work into a 12-hour day. You don't need to burn everything down—or rebuild from scratch.

You just need a better blueprint—a practical way to align your operations, finances, and team in a way that fits your reality.

This book won't ask you to master a hundred things at once—or force your business into a rigid framework. It's not about perfection. It's about momentum. It's about creating just enough structure to move forward without so much complexity that it slows you down.

The approach you'll find here blends financial clarity with operational strategy—grounded in how people actually work. You'll learn how to strengthen your systems and your margins—without losing the heart of your business in the process.

It's designed to meet you where you are, focus on what matters most, and move at a pace that works for you.

Because you don't have to do everything. But you do have to start.

Let's Get Started

If you've been doing everything right and still feel like it's not working, this book is for you.

Whether you see yourself as a CEO, a business owner, or somewhere in between, you're responsible for the health and future of your company.

This book will help you stop growing broke—and start growing profits, sustainability, and freedom.

The chapters ahead will show you how to transform a business that's growing broke into one that grows profitably and sustainably.

You'll learn how to spot the leaks that drain your cash, the bottlenecks dragging down your team, and the small shifts that will give you back your time, control, and peace of mind.

Once you've uncovered financial and operational clues that reveal what's not working, you'll apply the 5 Rules to Stop Growing Broke—a set of foundational principles for building a business that scales sustainably, profitably, and without burning you out.

With those principles in place, you'll learn to use the 5D Systematization Process to build sustainable systems that actually work for your team—and the AIM Loop to keep improving what matters most without adding unnecessary complexity.

You don't need to systematize everything overnight. You'll learn the key pieces, so you can choose where to start—and where to focus first. You'll see how a few smart systems— built intentionally— can outperform a thousand scattered fixes.

You're not building a business based on hustle and grit. You're building one with integrity—financial, structural, and team.

Let's start by unpacking what "growing broke" really means—and how to put an end to it once and for all.

From Insight to Action—The Tools to Make It Happen

You don't have to figure this out alone—or from scratch.

I've pulled together the key tools, visuals, and a free companion workbook to help you take action as you read.

You'll find everything at:

→ **Resources.StopGrowingBroke.com**

Prefer to scan? Use the QR code below to head straight to the page.

When Growing Broke Feels Like Success

You're selling more, the pace is quick,
But profit's thin—and cash runs slick.
The wins look good, the team feels proud,
Yet stress keeps rising through the crowd.

Beneath the buzz, the cracks expand—
No systems strong enough to stand.
You're not the problem—but here's the clue:
The growth won't hold without structure, too.

CHAPTER 1

When Growing Broke Feels Like "Success"

---

*"A business that makes nothing but money
is a poor business."*
— Henry Ford

When you're running a business, it makes sense to aim for growth: more clients, more revenue, more recognition. But somewhere along the way, what once felt exciting starts to feel exhausting. You might feel like Alex from the introduction. If you're wondering why success doesn't feel the way you thought it would, you're not broken—you're just running into problems that growth, i.e., revenue alone can't solve.

What If Growth Is the Problem?

The Hidden Gap Between Revenue and Reality

On paper, everything looks great. Revenue is higher than ever, clients are coming in, your team is growing, and everyone keeps telling you how successful you are. You may have even won an award or two—*Best Place to Work* or maybe *Top Five Businesses to Watch*.

But behind the scenes, you're struggling to keep it all together. Even though revenue is up, your stomach drops whenever it's time to pay invoices or payroll. It doesn't make any sense! Something is just not right, so you start to dig in.

You realize that the huge custom software project you delivered to a new client actually lost money. You had to hire contractors to meet the deadline, so your costs went up. Then, trying to impress the client, you threw in a bunch of little extras—eating into your margin. You know from experience that "gold-plating" is never a good idea, yet you did it anyway. And to top it off, scope creep kicked in when your team allowed the client to have three rounds of revisions instead of two.

"More money coming in doesn't mean more money staying in."

Once you figure out what happened, the shock, embarrassment, and disappointment start to creep in. You're intelligent, organized, and driven by a clear vision and mission. You have real-world experience. So how did you let this happen? It hasn't happened to any of your colleagues...has it?

That's where you're wrong.

Most CEOs and business owners run into the same problems and feel the same way, but no one wants to admit it, so everyone puts on a happy face and says everything is fine. You are not alone!

Revenue is an easy number to focus on. It's impressive. It's easy to share—and makes you sound successful—and it's easy to track. It feels good to say, "I finally joined the 2.5% of businesses that crossed the 7-figure mark!" But judging a business by its revenue is like deciding to buy a house based on the size of the front door without even having an inspection.

The sneaky thing about revenue is that it can easily cover up decreasing profit, increasing expenses, and operational inefficiencies. Higher revenue makes you feel like you're winning, even as the six-month emergency fund you saved up slowly dwindles and cash flow seems to be flowing more out than in!

The disconnect between revenue and reality is easy to miss— especially when things look busy and successful on the surface. But bringing in more business doesn't automatically mean things are getting better.

In fact, busy-ness itself can create the illusion of progress while masking deeper problems.

Busy ≠ Profitable: Stop Mistaking Motion for Progress

Even after you've pinpointed the financial leaks, another trap shows up—believing that staying busy means you're making real progress.

Many CEOs assume that if everyone is busy, they're productive and things are moving forward. But is that effort actually profitable? Is the work moving the team toward a deliverable or just spinning wheels? Is it supporting internal goals? Or is it truly just "busy work" that isn't providing value?

A full calendar and a long to-do list can look impressive—but that doesn't mean the work is creating value or generating profit.

Take a minute to check your own habits. Are you a CEO who checks parking lots at 5 p.m. to see who's still there? Do you assume someone is not working if you can't see them at their desk or see their green dot online?

Without clarity on where all the time and energy are actually going, it's easy to mistake movement for momentum while your profits quietly disappear.

So ask yourself: are you encouraging productive work, or just more busy work?

The Fear That Keeps You from Opening the Books

Even when you're not a "parking lot checker," it's tempting to believe that the busy-ness will "all even out" once you get the next big client or hit a certain revenue goal. But busy-ness without profitability scales the problems, not the profit.

If you're not paying attention, by the time you realize what's happening, the damage is already done—and difficult to recover from. When you don't know exactly what a project or client is costing you, it's easy to undercharge, over-deliver, or let profits erode without realizing it.

Over time, those tiny leaks drain profitability faster than most owners realize—until the margins are too thin to sustain growth, or maybe even the business.

And keep in mind—it's not just a math issue. It's a systems issue that shows up in your financials. Every late invoice, underpriced project, or stalled payment is a symptom of deeper operational gaps.

When I talk about systems, I don't mean tools, software, or automation. I'm talking about the structure behind the scenes— how work actually gets done, reliably and profitably, even when things get busy and you're not in the room.

Intellectually, you know you need to look at your financial reports. But you may avoid looking at them because now you're afraid of what you'll see. Is that stomachache starting to return? Or maybe you do look at them, but without knowing what you're looking at, it's hard to know what matters.

Cash flow statements, balance sheets, and profit and loss statements can seem like another language when you don't know how to read them or apply the information to your business. Is a profit of $20,000 good or bad? Is a profit margin of 12% good or bad? Is your debt-to-equity ratio really that important?

When decisions are made based on your gut instead of financial data, it's easy to underprice services, misjudge the necessary resources you'll need, and miss the early warning signs of trouble. Instinct is valuable, but without numbers to ground it, it's like driving a car blindfolded.

If you're reading this book, your business probably isn't big enough to have a chief financial officer—but you still need to understand (or get help understanding) your finances. Small financial problems grow into major ones. And the longer you wait, whether from fear or not understanding the issues, the fewer options you'll have for fixing them.

Managing with clear financial data creates stability, clarity, and the ability to make smarter, more confident moves even when things get tough.

That fear of facing the truth is understandable—but it's also what allows deeper financial problems to hide in plain sight.

The Red Flags Most CEOs Miss Until It's Too Late

So, what financial red flags should you be looking for? I've already alluded to a few, but now let's take a closer look at the warning signs that might be hiding in plain sight.

Growing Broke—The Profit Trap Behind Top-Line Growth

The big red flag is growing broke, i.e., increasing revenue and decreasing profits. You feel like your business is going like gangbusters, but profit margins are getting tighter. It feels like you're running faster just to stay in place, or—worse, running faster and flying off the back of the treadmill.

Additional costs from rework, smoothing things over with the client, or purchasing unplanned software or tools to meet a deadline all chip away at that built-in profit margin.

Without strong pricing, scope control, and effective finance and operations systems in place, growth—meaning more revenue—won't fix the problem—it only magnifies it. It's frustrating and exhausting—you feel like there's never enough left over to breathe. You're starting to feel a constant, underlying panic that no amount of hustle seems to fix.

"Top-line growth feels good until bottom-line reality hits you."

And tighter margins aren't the only warning sign hiding in plain sight.

Cash Flow Whiplash That Sabotages Growth

One month looks good, the next feels like a free fall. It's like being on a rollercoaster. Inconsistent billing practices, slow-paying clients, and big upfront expenses without getting paid by clients make cash flow wildly unpredictable and turn financial management into a nerve-wracking guessing game. Without a system to even it out, every month feels like financial roulette.

You haven't paid yourself for three months just to make sure there's enough money in the bank account to pay the bills. You certainly haven't taken any profit distributions for yourself, and you're considering applying for another business credit card or maybe even taking out a personal loan.

The cash flow rollercoaster keeps you stuck in survival mode, making short-term decisions out of fear, which almost always delays progress toward any long-term goals. And you have to pass on amazing opportunities simply because there's no cash to take advantage of them.

It gets even trickier when the money you *thought* you earned is stuck in projects still sitting in development.

Trapped Cash = Trouble

Another red flag that often gets missed—until it is impacting cash flow—is revenue trapped in unfinished work. Even though the sale is booked, no money comes in until key milestones are met— or the work is fully completed.

Delayed work means delayed payment. When it drags on too long, the inability to bill a client and get paid becomes a liability. You still need to pay your bills and make payroll, so cash reserves get drained, which leads to pressure on every part of the business.

It's also easy to underestimate just how much cash is tied up in unfinished work. Over time, the gap between billed revenue and collected revenue increases, leading to a serious cash crunch you never saw coming.

These are just a few of the red flags, but when you add up shrinking margins, the cash flow swings, and delayed revenue, no wonder so many businesses feel like they're running uphill just to keep pace. Without strong systems, every "win" silently drains your time, team, and cash flow instead of fueling real growth.

With the right financial systems in place, growth becomes strategic—not reactive. You can see which clients, services, or projects actually build profit instead of decreasing it. Every new deal strengthens the business instead of weakening it.

When you're already overwhelmed, it's tempting to look away instead of facing the financial truths—but you can't fix what you can't see.

Are you reaching for the antacid tablets?

Can't See It, Can't Fix It—Awareness Is Your Superpower

Facing the facts isn't easy—but it's the only way forward. Numbers aren't the enemy. In fact, they're the only things that can give you back control of your business.

Stop Wearing Chaos Like a Badge of Honor

Growth doesn't have to mean chaos, burnout, or living in survival mode. Survival mode isn't sustainable, and it's not healthy!

When you work 16+ hours a day to hold everything together, you may view it as proof of commitment or determination. But normalizing it turns survival mode into a lifestyle, which is not going to help you reach the goals you set when you started your business.

The challenges and struggles of a CEO are not uncommon—but they aren't inevitable, either. They're fixable, but only when you stop accepting the challenges and your current survival mode response as "normal." When chaos is accepted as the cost of growth, real issues—like poor systems, unclear priorities, and hidden inefficiencies—stay hidden. If you don't see chaos as a problem, you never look for a solution.

"When chaos feels normal, problems stay invisible."

But determination alone isn't enough—the real issue runs deeper than effort.

It's a Systems Issue, Not a Willpower Issue

Working 16+ hours a day isn't the answer. Hard work can carry a business only so far—then the cracks start to show. Growth is the test that reveals whether your business is structurally sound, ready to scale—and where the cracks are.

Without solid foundational systems, growth magnifies the cracks instead of creating stability. Growth exposes weak systems, and no amount of hustle can permanently patch over a missing foundation. Picture a crack in the sidewalk compared to the San Andreas Fault!

Strong systems create consistency, scalability, and resilience—things willpower alone can't provide and sustain. When systems hold the weight, the business stops depending on just you or a small team to power through.

The first step to solving any challenge isn't more hustle or throwing in some new technology. It's actually much simpler than either of those—it's awareness.

Awareness Is the First Step to Taking Back Control

Awareness is the first—and most powerful—step toward growing and scaling sustainably—because you can't fix what you can't (or won't) see. Once you recognize the real problems and stop reacting to symptoms, you can start addressing the root causes.

True control doesn't come from working harder, but from clearly seeing what's broken and choosing to build better foundational systems. When you solve the real issues and stop just putting out fires, you can get off the hamster wheel and start building momentum that's actually sustainable.

Revenue growth can cover a lot of cracks, but it doesn't create real stability. And eventually, those cracks will be exposed. Chaos isn't a prerequisite for success. Missing family time and canceling vacations aren't proof that you're doing it right.

Seeing the numbers clearly—and facing what's really happening—is the first step toward taking back control and building a business that you run rather than your business running you.

In the next chapter, we'll dig into more signs and symptoms that may be quietly pulling your business down if you're not looking for them—and how to start fixing them.

When Busy-ness Becomes a Business Risk

You run the show, you take the lead—
But every win creates new need.
Each task, each call, runs back through you—
No time to think, just push on through.

The team's not weak—they're underused.
Without clear lanes, they stay confused.
It's not more hands that makes things stick—
It's structure that creates the click.

CHAPTER 2

When Busy-ness Becomes a Business Risk

"You can do anything, but not everything."
— David Allen

Not all business problems show up in a spreadsheet.

In Chapter 1, we looked at the hidden financial risks that creep in when you don't have a strong systems foundation. But before the numbers take a hit, the cracks usually show up in your time, your team, and your day-to-day operations. And remember, when I say *systems*, I don't mean tools or software—I mean the structure behind how things actually get done.

Let's look at these areas to see what to be on the lookout for.

No Off Switch

When the business relies too heavily on you, there's no real separation between your role and the business's success. You're not just running the business—you are the business. And that doesn't leave room for strategic growth, stability, or breathing.

Being in constant reaction mode isn't a reflection of your leadership—it's the result of the business's dependence on you. The key is to shift your mindset from "I need to work harder" to "The systems need to work better."

Chief Everything Officer Isn't a Strategy

It feels like no matter how capable your team is, every unresolved issue still finds its way back to you. You're not just running the business—you *are* the business. Instead of focusing on strategy, vision, or growth, you're stuck in the role of Chief Everything Officer. From client requests to team questions and tech glitches, it all lands on your desk.

At first, it might feel efficient. You know the business better than anyone. You can make quick decisions. You can fix things faster than you can explain how to fix them. But over time, that automatic "just let me do it" response becomes a trap. It creates a hidden dependency: slowing decisions, hampering team growth, and reinforcing a structure that requires your involvement in everything.

You know you should delegate, but without strong systems in place, it feels risky. If there's no clear way to track expectations or confirm quality work, handing something off often means you'll have to double-check it later anyway. So the easiest path becomes doing it yourself—even when you're exhausted, overcommitted, and behind on the strategic side of running the business.

The more hats you wear, the less time you have to reinforce the foundation. Instead of being the architect, you're the handyman, and the vicious cycle continues.

The more this dynamic plays out, the more your business becomes built around what's in your head—rather than around systems that make success repeatable without you. What starts as a practical workaround becomes a structural weakness—a hidden flaw that limits scalability.

When everything runs through you, you're not the only one losing time—you're also limiting the ability of the business to generate and sustain value. The business can only go as far and as fast as you can.

Stuck in Reaction Mode—Again

You want to be the CEO—Chief *Executive* Officer, not Chief *Everything* Officer. Not the project manager, the help desk rep, and the admin rolled into one. But when everything feels urgent, there's never time to step back and look at the bigger picture.

"You can't outwork a broken system."

Strategic projects, process improvements, and proactive planning always seem to get pushed to "next month" or "after this launch." Then the next crisis hits, and once again, the important work gets sidelined by the urgent and moves farther down the to-do list.

Without protected time to step back and design the business to scale, you stay stuck in a loop: react, resolve, repeat.

You're not lazy or undisciplined. The business has simply trained everyone—including you—to prioritize what's loudest, not what's most important.

The hidden cost of this urgency is huge. Projects that could reduce rework, increase client retention, or improve profitability never even get off the ground. Initiatives that would lighten your load or give your team more autonomy stay stuck in limbo because there's no time to implement them. Momentum? It evaporates every time you have to stop and put out another fire.

Eventually, you may start to wonder...

What If You're the Bottleneck?

You can see it happening. Projects come to a grinding halt waiting for your sign-off. The team hesitates to make decisions without your input. You're the common denominator in every delay—and it's starting to feel unsustainable.

You want your team to take more initiative, but without clear guidelines and expectations, mistakes are bound to happen—and they can be costly. You're stuck in a painful catch-22: overwhelmed by how much relies on you, but unsure how to step back without things falling apart.

The fear of letting go is real, especially when you've been burned before. But as long as you remain the gatekeeper for everything, your business stays fragile. It's not just your schedule at risk—it's your reputation, your clients' experiences, and your team's trust in the process.

As Peter Drucker said, "The bottleneck is always at the top of the bottle." The longer you stay at the center of everything, the more you limit your business's ability to grow beyond you.

Let's not forget the financial side. When the business can't move without you, your growth—and your income—become directly tied to your availability. That's a risky equation. You also expose the business to risk: a family emergency, a health issue, or even a well-deserved vacation can stop progress. If you're the only one who can truly keep things moving, every absence becomes a liability, and every growth spurt threatens to break the system.

If things still aren't moving—despite your best efforts—it's not a leadership issue; it's a systems issue. That means the real opportunity isn't about doing more—it's about designing better.

Am I the Bottleneck? Quick Quiz

Check all that apply:

- ☐ You're the go-to for questions or decisions— even on things you didn't realize were still on your plate.
- ☐ You find yourself answering the same questions again and again.
- ☐ You feel uneasy handing off work without double-checking it.
- ☐ Projects or clients stall when you're out sick or take time off.
- ☐ You're the only one who knows how certain things get done.

If you checked three or more...

You're not alone—but it's a sign the business is still relying on you—not on systems.

Try this: Start with one small, repeatable task. Work with your team to turn it into a basic checklist or mini-process—just enough to take it off your plate. Then step back and let your people run it for a week or two.

What works, what doesn't, and what gets missed will show you exactly where the system needs reinforcement. That's where you improve—not by doing it yourself, but by strengthening what supports your team.

Blame the System—Not the People

When things start slipping—deadlines, quality, client satisfaction—it's tempting to assume your team is the problem. Maybe they aren't taking the initiative. Maybe they aren't as strong as you hoped. Maybe it's a hiring issue.

But in most cases, the issue isn't a people problem—it's a systems problem. Your team isn't underperforming because they don't care. They're underperforming because the business hasn't given them what they need to succeed: structure, clarity, and consistency.

When Your Team Can't Move Without You

You've hired smart, capable people. But even strong teams hesitate without clear decision-making frameworks or shared expectations.

They want to move faster and take ownership, but when responsibilities are unclear and there's no playbook to follow, people default to caution. They're not sure where their authority begins or ends, and the risk of guessing wrong feels too high. So instead of stepping up, they wait.

That kind of hesitation doesn't mean your team lacks motivation. It means they're trying to operate in an environment that hasn't set them up to succeed.

Meanwhile, you're pushing forward as best you can—but every time you step in, progress slows. Not because your team isn't capable, but because the system hasn't shown them how to move forward without you.

When that happens, everyone's out of sync. People aren't on the same page because—honestly—there is no page.

Inconsistency Is Slowing You Down

One client raves about your team. The next seems frustrated. And you're not quite sure why.

The quality of deliverables varies depending on who's involved. Client experience looks different from one project to the next. Internally, the team is operating more on memory and assumptions than on shared standards. There's no clear definition of "done," no baseline for quality, and no consistent rhythm for how work flows.

It turns out your team doesn't know what to do—or how to do it well. Without documented processes and expectations, quality becomes a moving target. When quality is open to interpretation, it's also open to variation, which is something your clients do notice, even if your team doesn't.

The result? Slower delivery, more rework, and rising frustration for everyone. This inconsistency not only affects client satisfaction—it also creates internal tension, missed deadlines, and costly rework that eats up time and trust. Your team starts second-guessing themselves, and you start wondering why everything takes longer than it should, even though everyone's trying their best.

That growing frustration and inconsistency was exactly the turning point for Priya, the CEO of a boutique web design studio. Her clients loved the creativity and strategy behind her firm's work— but recently, one project ran weeks late, and another missed key features from the scope.

The issue wasn't talent—her team was smart and experienced. Each project was being run differently. There was no shared playbook, no checklist, and no central process for moving deliverables from draft to done.

After one unhappy client nearly walked, Priya spent a weekend documenting her team's core process and creating a simple "pre-launch" checklist. Within one month, revisions dropped by half, and client feedback scores went up. It wasn't about controlling her team—it was about giving them the structure they needed to support quality.

"Our creativity didn't change," she said, *"but our consistency did— and that's what made the biggest difference."*

Team Frustration Is a Signal—Not a Flaw

At first glance, it might look like disengagement. Missed details, repeated questions, dropped handoffs—it's easy to assume someone's checked out, doesn't care, or just isn't the right fit.

But often, what looks like underperformance or disengagement is really a response to uncertainty. People want to do good work, but when they operate in an environment without structure, they start to back off. That hesitation isn't due to a lack of talent or motivation—it's because they don't know what showing up successfully even looks like.

Low morale, turnover, and passive resistance aren't character flaws—they're symptoms. They often point to missing systems—unclear roles, inconsistent standards, or leadership rhythms that shift with every fire that needs putting out.

People want to succeed, but when the environment doesn't support success, even high performers start to disengage.

When you start losing key players, you don't just lose institutional knowledge. You lose momentum. You lose client continuity. You spend more time hiring, retraining, and backfilling. Not only is there a toll on your time and your team's energy, but there is also a very real toll on your finances.

Left unmanaged, team dysfunction quietly zaps profit. Rework eats up billable hours. Missed expectations cost you referrals. Repeated turnover drives up your hiring, training, and onboarding costs. All of these add up to slower delivery, hits to your reputation, and even more chaos.

"Great people can't thrive in broken systems."

Chaos Isn't Culture—It's a Warning Sign

A little chaos is easy to dismiss, especially in a business that's growing. But over time, what begins as scrappy survival mode quietly becomes the default operating model. Before you know it, chaos stops being the exception and becomes the expectation.

When that happens, your business begins running on sheer effort instead of a solid foundation.

Scaling Without Systems = Scaling Chaos

More clients. More revenue. More team members.

But also? More moving parts. More confusion. More inconsistency. More stress.

Growth without systems doesn't reduce the chaos and strain—it amplifies it. Adding people or projects without strengthening the foundation doesn't solve overwhelm; it multiplies it. You end up with more complexity without more stability.

Every time you grow without tightening your processes, you're layering complexity on top of an already wobbly structure. It starts to feel like the more successful you become, the more fragile the business becomes. Why? Because you're not scaling clarity—you're scaling chaos.

And when you're scaling chaos, even your wins come with warning signs—team stress, messy handoffs, and missed deadlines. You're achieving more, but holding it all together starts to feel harder than ever.

Heroic Effort Won't Hold Forever

In the absence of clear systems, the business ends up leaning on people instead, especially your most dependable team members. These are the ones who always jump in, figure things out, stay late to fill the gaps, and make sure deadlines are met.

They're not just high performers—they're your unofficial safety net. But when a business relies on heroic effort instead of reliable systems, that safety net starts to wear thin. Even your A-team can't hold everything together forever. They start showing signs of strain—missed details, delayed responses, growing frustration. Or worse, they leave.

And when they do, everything slows down. Institutional knowledge disappears, projects backslide, and clients feel the impact.

"Hustle and grit can't hold it all together."

Building a business around human effort instead of structural integrity is a short-term solution with long-term costs. You're not just risking performance—you're risking burnout, turnover, and instability exactly when you're trying to scale. Not a good combination.

Built on Firefighting, Not Foundations

When every day is shaped by what's urgent, unpredictability becomes the norm. You're not just reacting to a few fires—you're running a business that's structurally unprepared for growth.

You can't steer the business when you're stuck chasing dropped balls. You're solving issues instead of preventing them. You can't scale a business on urgency and instinct. Without systems, even success becomes fragile.

It's easy to think the chaos will fade once you hit your next revenue goal or hire the right person. But growth doesn't fix what's broken—it magnifies it.

What holds your business together tomorrow won't be the next win. It will be the systems you build today.

In the next chapter, we'll connect the dots between these operational symptoms and their financial consequences and unpack why the real risk isn't growing—it's growing broke.

The Real Risk Isn't Growing, It's Growing Broke

The sales look strong, the pace is high—
But profits slip and cash runs dry.
The more you sell, the less you bank—
And stress runs high when profits tank.

The red flags rise—late pay, scope creep—
But deeper still, the cracks run deep.
It's not always bad luck or pricing flaws—
It's often broken systems as the cause.

CHAPTER 3

The Real Risk Isn't Growing, It's Growing Broke

*"The system you have is perfectly designed to give
you the results you're getting."*
— W. Edwards Deming

Growth is supposed to make things easier: more revenue, a bigger team, better tools—all signs that your business is heading in the right direction.

But here's the part no one talks about: when the systems underneath aren't strong enough, growth doesn't ease the pressure—it multiplies it. What looks like success on the surface can quietly lead to financial strain that's anything but sustainable.

What Got You Here Won't Get You There

At a certain point in business, the playbook that once felt like your superpower starts working against you. What used to be your edge—your ability to jump in, move fast, and carry a heavy load—now feels more like a weakness than a strength. In fact, you may be tempted to toss the playbook altogether!

You haven't changed. Your standards haven't dropped. But the stakes have risen. The complexity has increased. And the cracks in the foundation that were manageable at $500K or even $1M are now louder, wider, and more expensive to ignore.

That's not a sign of failure—it's a sign you've outgrown your current way of operating.

What's tricky is that the early-stage habits that helped build momentum are hard to shake. You care deeply. You've always been the one who makes things happen. You've always found a way to push through. But when you're leading a team and delivering at scale, those same habits start reinforcing the very problems you're trying to solve.

So, what happens when you keep pushing with an old playbook in a business that's already outgrown it?

Growth Exposes the Cracks

In the early days, cobbling things together worked fine. If a client needed a quick turnaround, you made it happen. If a team member had a question, they came straight to you. Processes were loose, but the business was small enough that you could get away with it—until growth changed that equation.

Now, each new client, project, and hire adds another layer of complexity. And those cracks in the foundation you used to jump over? They're widening—fast.

Suddenly, a missed deadline isn't just a little hiccup—it's a lost client. A team handoff gone sideways means rework—not just redoing a slide deck, but burning through hours that were supposed to be billable. Just a little scope creep, and suddenly the whole project starts losing profit.

Even when things look fine on the surface, you can feel the strain underneath. That low-grade hum of "We're one dropped ball away from a major client issue," or "I'm not sure how much more we can take on without something slipping."

It's not that the team isn't trying. It's not that you're not leading. It's that your system—or lack of one—can't support the increased work.

Here's where it gets risky. Initially, when cracks multiply, the business doesn't slow down. Sometimes, it grows faster—with more revenue and more clients. But growth also brings more moving parts, and it starts to feel like it's all being held up by a wobbly foundation on the San Andreas Fault.

That's not a hustle problem—it's a structural integrity problem.

Same Effort, Worse Results

You haven't stopped working hard. In fact, you're probably putting in more hours now than ever. You're pouring in time, energy, attention, and care—doing everything you used to do, and then some, but it's still not enough. Something has shifted.

The results don't match the effort.

You fix one problem, and three more pop up—like a game of whack-a-mole. You push a big project across the finish line, and cash is still tight. You finally land that dream client, and the not-so-dreamy delivery nearly breaks your team and leaves you with a dissatisfied one.

It's deeply disheartening. You're doing all the things that used to work. But instead of building momentum, it feels like you're running on a treadmill that keeps speeding up—while you stay in the same place.

Then you start second-guessing everything. You're doing what worked before—but now, it's not working. That's the real signal that something deeper needs to change. Because when consistent effort no longer delivers consistent results, it's not an effort problem—it's a structural one.

The business isn't broken. You're not broken. But the way you're operating? It's not built for where you are now—or where you're headed next.

"More effort won't fix a system that's no longer built for where you're headed."

If the foundation isn't strong enough to support where you're going, it doesn't just slow you down—it starts to cost you. At first, it shows up as rising team tension, delivery that feels harder than it should, and a nagging sense that the wheels are about to come off. Left unchecked, those cracks lead to mounting financial pressure— disappearing profit, clunky cash flow, and a client experience that starts to suffer. You're no longer just stretched thin—you're growing broke. So what does that look like?

What Growing Broke Really Looks Like

Sometimes, the warning signs of a business growing broke are loud and obvious. But more often, they're subtle—easy to explain away and easy to miss until it's too late. That's what makes growing broke so sneaky—and so costly. On the outside, everything still looks good. Revenue is up. Clients are coming in. The team is busy. But underneath, the business is running on fumes.

Let's look at a few of the signs that you're growing broke—or are on your way there.

Revenue Up, Profits Down

Sales are climbing, but your bank account doesn't reflect it. You're working harder, serving more clients, and closing bigger deals—but the profits just aren't there. It feels like you're moving forward, yet financially, you're spinning your wheels.

You start analyzing your sales cycle and double-checking your pricing model, wondering if you missed something in your cost estimates. But then you dig into the numbers and realize the problem isn't revenue—it's that profit is quietly leaking out of the sides.

Every underestimated proposal, every internal delay that ate up hours, every new piece of software that was never fully implemented, every "extra" you threw in to keep a client happy—it all adds up.

You're not losing money because the work isn't there. You're losing money because the business isn't structured to protect profit as it grows.

Falling Profit, Rising Panic

Cash flow becomes a constant guessing game. You delay vendor payments. Running payroll sends you reaching for the Tums. You haven't paid yourself in months.

Then an opportunity comes up—someone great you'd love to hire, a conference you want to attend, a tool that could streamline operations—and you have to pass. Not because it's the wrong move, but because there's no money to make it.

Here is what growing broke really looks like: more sales, more activity, more strain—and that three-month emergency fund in the bank disappeared months ago. Even small bumps in the road now feel like the Rocky Mountains. Every opportunity becomes a missed one. You're working too hard to be this financially fragile.

5 Signs You're Growing Broke

You're bringing in revenue—but it's not translating into financial stability. Here are five signs your business may be growing broke—even if it looks successful on the surface.

1. Revenue is rising—but profits are flat or falling.
   You're selling more but keeping less—and you're not exactly sure where the money is going.
2. You've delayed paying yourself (or your vendors) more than twice this quarter.
   You're covering everyone else—but it's starting to take a personal toll.
3. You're saying no to smart opportunities—because there's no cash to fund them.
   The right hire, the right tool, or the right conference keeps getting pushed down the road.
4. Key clients don't come back—and you're not sure why.
   Renewals, referrals, and long-term loyalty are becoming harder to earn.
5. You can't explain your cost per project or client without guessing.

   If your numbers aren't clear, profit is leaking somewhere—and you likely don't even see it.

Broken Systems, Broken Bottom Line

At this stage, delivery starts breaking down. Rework creeps in—communication slips. Handoffs get missed. Team members are over capacity, but there's no time to fix the system, so you just keep pushing.

And that's when profit takes another hit.

You're losing billable hours to cleanup work. You're refunding clients or absorbing the scope you should've billed for. You're paying twice for the same work—once to complete it, and once to correct it.

Then the ripple becomes a tidal wave. One of your A-players quits. A client opts out of Phase 2. A vendor suddenly changes your payment terms—and not in your favor.

Mild chaos is quietly turning into a financial nightmare.

When Clients Go, Growth Slows

Earlier, we talked about how growth doesn't slow right away when the cracks start to multiply. But when the number and size of the cracks reach a tipping point, you officially move into growing broke territory. When you're growing broke, client experiences usually go south—not because your team doesn't care—but because the cracks are too deep to cover up anymore.

Clients begin to feel the cracks—service becomes inconsistent, and their confidence begins to fade.

Clients stop referring, and they don't return. Every new month starts from zero, and acquiring new business is expensive.

Losing clients doesn't just sting—it stalls your momentum. And not in the "finally, a breather" kind of way. This kind of slowdown makes everything harder.

You can't rely on loyalty, word of mouth, or retention— because even your best efforts are being undermined by the very systems that are meant to support your growth.

You don't have a marketing problem. You have a systems problem—and it's costing you real money.

The longer these problems go unaddressed, the more they intensify—team morale dips. Client trust erodes—financial stress mounts. Eventually, you're no longer just managing stress—you're trying to recover from real damage.

The Cost of Waiting

When you're deep in the day-to-day, it's easy to convince yourself that things will settle down soon—after this project, after this quarter, after this hire. The truth is, waiting doesn't just cost you time—it costs you options.

What once felt like a small issue now has ripple effects across your business—and your bottom line. The longer you delay addressing the cracks, the deeper they spread—and the harder (and more expensive) they are to repair. Ignore the cracks long enough, and you're not just fixing problems—you're rebuilding from the ground up.

> *"The longer you wait, the fewer options you have—and the harder the fix becomes."*

You don't just lose time. You lose leverage, capacity, and control.

When Quick Fixes Become Expensive Failures

At first, the band-aids seemed to work. You pushed off deadlines, shuffled responsibilities, hired a contractor, or offered a discount. At the time, none of it felt like a big deal.

But over time, those "temporary" fixes start snowballing—until they become an avalanche.

You miss key details because you're still relying on memory instead of process. You lose your biggest account over a preventable mistake. What once felt like agility now feels like instability.

These aren't just minor annoyances anymore—they're risks to your reputation, your revenue, and your client retention. And the longer the business runs in duct-tape mode, the more likely it is that one of those cracks will become the break that you can't bounce back from.

No Data, No Clarity—Just Survival

As the chaos builds, it chips away at your ability to lead with clarity. You lack the data you need to make decisions. You don't have the space to think clearly.

Char learned this the hard way.

Char's team had grown quickly—but her systems hadn't. She was fielding questions from all sides, juggling shifting deadlines, unclear priorities, and scattered financial data while doing it. When a client asked for a discount on a delayed project, Char hesitated. She didn't know how many hours had gone into the work, or what it had actually cost to deliver. Without a dashboard or clean data, she had to go with her gut. Weeks later she realized the project had already lost money.

It's a familiar pattern—especially when the numbers aren't clear and the clock is ticking.

You default to what's loudest, what's fastest, or what feels safest in the moment—even if it pulls you off course.

Vision takes a back seat to survival.

Instead of building for the next phase, you're scrambling to survive the next invoice cycle. You put off strategic hires. You pass on smart investments you know would pay off. You're not resisting progress—you just lack the visibility or capacity to move forward with confidence.

Without structure or clarity, even good decisions feel like guesses. That's when leadership starts to slip—not because you don't care, but because you're flying blind. No dashboard. No map. Not even a reliable rearview mirror.

The Turning Point

Eventually, you realize that what got you here won't get you there. That's not just a milestone—it's the turning point.

Admitting it doesn't mean you've failed. Quite the opposite—it means you're ready to lead more strategically.

The problem isn't that the business is too complicated or that you're not cut out for growth. The issue is that the way you've been operating—while it got you this far—can't take you the rest of the way. And the longer you ignore it, the worse things are going to get.

The good news? You're not at a dead end—you're at a turning point.

Recognizing it means your business is ready for a stronger, more flexible foundation—one that doesn't rely on hustle, heroics, or the hope that things will somehow work themselves out.

It's time to commit—to stop growing broke and start building smarter. You'll feel the shift. Not because it magically gets easier, but because now you're solving the right problem.

In the next chapter, we'll walk through the 5 Rules to Stop Growing Broke—and show you how to start building a business that's profitable, scalable, and sustainable from the inside out.

The 5 Rules to Stop Growing Broke

You've added people, stacked new tech,
But the cracks are still there—what the heck?!
Growth can't rest on guess-and-go—
It needs a frame that holds the flow.

Five rules to build what won't collapse:
Start with systems. Skip the traps.
Simplify first. Then scale with care.
The path to profit starts right there.

CHAPTER 4

The 5 Rules to Stop Growing Broke

"You do not rise to the level of your goals.
You fall to the level of your systems."
—James Clear

What's your first instinct when your to-do list is longer than your arm and everyone needs something from you now?

Do you do more, work later, and power through? Or do you hire more people and buy better software?

If you're anything like most CEOs, you've tried all of the above and then some. You care about your team, your clients, and your reputation. So when things start breaking down, you jump in and try to patch it all together with duct tape, sweat, and sheer determination.

Because that's what you've always done—and it's worked... until now.

I've said it before, but I'll say it again: real growth doesn't come from pushing harder. It comes from building smarter.

Most businesses that feel chaotic on the surface are missing something underneath—a strong, well-designed structure. The systems that should hold everything together either don't exist, don't work, or aren't followed. It's like trying to build a second story before pouring the foundation.

This chapter introduces the *5 Rules to Stop Growing Broke*—a framework for building a business that can scale sustainably, profitably, and without running you into the ground. These Rules aren't trendy hacks—they're foundational principles that, when followed, will change everything about how you lead, grow, and regain control.

But first, let's look at why all your past fixes haven't worked.

Fix the Real Problem—Not Just the Symptoms

We've been taught to treat the symptoms—more tools, more people, more effort. But if you want real change, you need to look beneath the surface—at the foundation, the systems that support your operations. I'm talking about the backbone of your business— how work gets done profitably, reliably, and without triggering cash flow chaos every time things get busy.

"If you're fixing the wrong problem, no amount of effort will get you out of the chaos."

Most Fixes Only Hide the Real Issues

When chaos hits, the go-to response is to throw resources at it: more staff, more meetings, more tools. But if you're solving surface symptoms instead of root causes, you'll just end up frustrated—and right back where you started. The symptoms might quiet down for a while, but the underlying instability is still there—waiting to resurface the next time things get busy.

That's because what looks like a productivity problem is usually a systems problem in disguise.

You're not falling behind because you're lazy or disorganized. You've probably tried every time management tip, project tracking tool, and delegation strategy out there. But without structured, repeatable systems behind the scenes, it feels like Groundhog Day—solving the same problems over and over again, hoping this time something sticks. And that's not sustainable.

If your business feels like a never-ending game of catch-up, it's not because you're not capable. It's because the foundation wasn't built to carry the load you're placing on it now. But we can fix that—starting with the 5 Rules to Stop Growing Broke that every sustainable, scalable business needs to follow.

The 5 Rules to Stop Growing Broke

These Rules aren't just suggestions—they're the essential structural principles for any business that wants to scale *without* sacrificing quality, profitability, or sanity. Each Rule builds on the last, and together, they form the mindset and systems you need to reclaim control and unlock growth—without costing you everything.

"Systems aren't a nice-to-have—they stop growth from becoming a liability."

If you're still spending more time reacting than leading… if your team is constantly behind despite their best efforts… and if every fix seems to break something else—it's time to stop tweaking and start transforming.

It's time for a better system, not just a better to-do list.

The 5 Rules to Stop Growing Broke

1. **Adopt a Systems-First Mindset** – Structure before tactics.
2. **Build and Streamline Core Systems First** – Consistency beats complexity.
3. **Avoid the Quick-Fix Tech Trap** – Technology can't fix chaos.
4. **Slow Down to Speed Up** – Structure first, then scale.
5. **Supercharge for Sustainability** – Optimize, automate, and elevate what already works.

Rule 1: Adopt a Systems-First Mindset

Success starts with a fundamental mindset shift. Your business isn't struggling because you need better tools—it's struggling because you lack strong systems. If you're constantly putting out fires, and every new hire or client only adds to the chaos, the issue isn't growth—it's the lack of a structured way to manage it.

Most CEOs start by reaching for tactics—efficiency hacks, tighter schedules, new software, longer hours. But if you don't understand how work should flow through your business, those quick fixes only speed up dysfunction. Can your team follow clear, repeatable steps, or does everything still require you to step in? Can a new employee get up to speed quickly—or is crucial knowledge locked in people's heads? Before anything else, clarity and structure have to come first.

Adopting a systems-first mindset means asking: "How should this process work every time?" "What would make this effortless for my team and clients?"

This mindset is likely the foundation your business has been missing. Strong systems don't just make things run more smoothly—they help you spend smarter, forecast better, and make decisions rooted in structure, not stress.

Rule 2: Build and Streamline Core Systems First

It's tempting to jump right into process improvement and optimization—but you can't refine what doesn't exist.

The first step isn't making things better or faster—it's making things *consistent*. Start with the high-impact areas that shape your client experience, revenue flow, and delivery quality.

Ask yourself:

- How does work move through the business from start to finish?
- Where do things get stuck, skipped, or miscommunicated?
- Where are the rework, delays, and scope creep that drain profitability?
- What must happen for a client to get great results—every time?

If onboarding new clients depends on one team member remembering every detail, that's not a system—it's a gamble. But with a simple, repeatable checklist and shared responsibility, client experience improves, team confidence rises, and fewer things fall through the cracks. A "system" or "process" doesn't have to be complicated—it just has to be consistent and keep everyone moving forward.

"Systems turn chaos into clarity—and clarity into control."

Until the process is clear, adding tools or handing off work will only multiply the mess. Don't rush to add tech or start delegating—at least, not yet. First, define the system—then build a solid foundation for your business needs. Once the work is clear—then, and only then—should you build efficiencies into it. When your systems are consistent, your numbers become more predictable—and that's when the financial clarity starts to show up.

This is where clarity becomes currency.

Rule 3: Avoid the Quick Fix Technology Trap

Technology isn't a substitute for structure—it's a force multiplier. If you layer tech onto a broken process, you just amplify the chaos.

Many CEOs fall into the trap of thinking a better CRM, project management tool, or AI will solve their problems. But tools are only as good as the systems they support. If your team isn't clear on who's supposed to do what, when, or how, no tool will save you.

Have you ever rolled out a new platform only to find—

- Nobody uses it?
- It adds more work?
- It creates even more confusion?

That's not a tech problem—that's a systems problem. Broken processes don't just create confusion—they drain profit. Every tool layered on top of inefficiency eats into profit and creates hidden costs that grow over time.

Rule 4: Slow Down to Speed Up

The pressure to scale quickly is real. But fast growth without strong systems isn't scaling—it's spiraling. True scaling means your business grows without sacrificing profit, sanity, or time.

This Rule is about intentional growth—slowing down just enough to make smart decisions, stabilize systems, and empower your team. Instead of rushing and patching as you go, take a step back and reinforce how things work. That's when everything moves faster—not from hustle, but from structure.

You can't shortcut structure. It's like skipping rebar in concrete—it might look fine, but it won't hold up under pressure.

Rule 5: Supercharge Systems for Sustainability and Impact

Once your core systems are stable, it's time to optimize. *Then* automate. *Then* elevate.

Now, tools and tech become valuable— not as band-aids, but as enhancers of what already works. You're not adding complexity—you're multiplying capacity. Real-time dashboards, automation tools, and documented standard operating procedures—these things will allow you to scale without losing control. These systems also give you measurable insights, so financial decisions aren't based on gut feel, but grounded in real data.

The goal isn't just survival. It's a business that thrives—where you're no longer the bottleneck, and where growth *adds* freedom instead of stealing it.

From Bottleneck to Two-Week Vacation

After years of growing revenue without a rise in profits, Maya, founder of a boutique HR consulting firm, hit a wall. Her team was skilled, and her services were in demand, but everything still ran through her.

She started with a mindset shift: her job wasn't to be the fixer—it was to build systems that solved problems without her.

Over the next few months, she focused on:

- ✓ Mapping out core delivery systems
- ✓ Streamlining project handoffs
- ✓ Improving the client experience
- ✓ Canceling unnecessary tech subscriptions
- ✓ Stabilizing key processes and internal systems
- ✓ Setting up a simple dashboard with a few key financial metrics, she now reviews monthly with her team

Today, Maya leads with intention—instead of chasing the next urgent thing. She has visibility into her numbers, trust in her team, and—for the first time in years—just took a two-week vacation without checking email once.

These five Rules might not sound revolutionary—but they're the reason other solutions haven't worked. You've probably tried hiring, hustling, or layering on more tools—only to find that each fix adds complexity instead of clarity.

That's because you've been trying to build growth on top of a shaky foundation.

These Rules are different. They don't just improve operations—they help stabilize cash flow, protect profit margins, and make sure growth doesn't come at the cost of your sanity.

In the next section, we'll look at why skipping this foundation is the reason you're still stuck—and how embracing it unlocks the kind of growth that finally feels sustainable.

No Foundation, No Future

Once you adopt the 5 Rules to Stop Growing Broke and begin building the structure your business has been missing, everything starts to click. You've likely been relying on effort, instinct, or workarounds—but now, you're building on something solid. And that changes everything.

Why Most Solutions Don't Stick

Hiring, marketing, and tech—none of it works the way it should when the foundation is missing. That's why even well-intentioned fixes so often fall flat. You buy a new tool, but no one uses it. You hire, but onboarding is a mess. You launch a new offer, but delivery is inconsistent.

You weren't doing it wrong—you were just doing it out of order.

Growth Didn't Break It—It Just Exposed the Cracks

Early on, you can get away without documented processes or clean handoffs. But as your business grows—especially if it grows quickly—those small gaps turn into serious liabilities. The cracks that used to be manageable suddenly become major breakdowns.

Growth didn't create the chaos—it just revealed what was already fragile or missing. Sales and marketing didn't break your business. They just turned up the volume on every flaw in your systems.

This Is How You Finally Move Forward

When you build on this foundation, you stop spinning your wheels. Your team gains clarity, your clients get consistency, and your numbers start to stabilize.

It's not magic—it's structure. And while you don't have to systematize every part of your business overnight—in fact, you shouldn't—you do need to commit to the 5 Rules to Stop Growing Broke. It's time to stop relying on duct tape and heroic effort to hold things together.

These Rules are your new foundation—your blueprint—whether you move quickly or take it one step at a time.

"The 5 Rules to Stop Growing Broke are the difference between mayhem and momentum."

Following them is how you finally scale with confidence, clarity, and control. Skipping them is why businesses stay stuck.

When implementing the 5 Rules to Stop Growing Broke, it's easy to focus only on operational systems—but operations alone won't solve everything. Without financial visibility, you can't scale sustainably—because you don't know what's really working, or what's quietly draining profit behind the scenes.

That's why finances can't be an afterthought. They're a key part of your larger system. When they're disconnected, it's like the right hand doesn't know what the left hand is doing—you lose clarity, precision, and control.

In the next chapter, we'll explore where hidden cash slips through the cracks—and how spotting those profit leaks helps reveal which systems need your attention next.

The Cash Clues that Change Everything

The numbers speak—but only when you listen.
Ignore the signs, and profit's what you're missin'.
Unpaid invoices, rising spend—
Hidden cash leaks won't self-amend.

It's not just math—it's systems too.
And each finance clue points out what to do.
Track the signs, then dig beneath—
That's how to stop the cashflow grief.

CHAPTER 5

The Cash Clues That Change Everything

"Revenue is vanity, profit is sanity, and cash is king."
— Alan Miltz

Now that you've seen the 5 Rules to Stop Growing Broke, it's time to get more specific about where to begin.

For most business owners, the fastest way to make real progress isn't a marketing campaign or a new offer. It's finding and fixing the cash leaks already hiding inside the business.

This chapter is about visibility—because you can't fix what you can't see. Most businesses have money slipping through the cracks. The difference is whether or not you're paying attention to what the numbers are trying to say.

We'll walk through key areas where cash tends to get stuck or lost, but we're not stopping there. These numbers aren't just financial metrics—they're clues that point directly to broken or missing systems that affect not just your profitability, but also your team's performance and your peace of mind.

Behind the Numbers—What Growing Broke Really Tells You

Growing broke happens when revenue increases but profits shrink—making the business harder to manage, not easier. On paper, things look good. But financially and operationally, something isn't adding up.

That's what growing broke looks like. So what can you do about it?

Growing Broke = A Warning Sign, Not a Failure

Growing broke is a signal that something underneath the surface isn't working. And the only way to move forward is to figure out *where* things are breaking down—and why.

You don't need to become a financial expert to fix growing broke. You just need to know what to watch for, what it's telling you, and where to start. The goal here isn't to obsess over financial reports—it's to use them as a roadmap, so you can solve the right problems, in the right order, and move forward with confidence.

> **The Numbers Looked Fine—Until They Didn't**
>
> Jordan, the CEO of a growing video production agency, didn't think anything was wrong financially. The project calendar was full, clients were happy, and revenue was steady. But payroll was always a nail-biter—and no one could explain where the cash was going.

It wasn't until Jordan started asking better questions—about gross profit, project overruns, and payment timing—that the picture became clearer. Too much was being spent on last-minute gear rentals. Invoices were going out late. And scope creep on deliverables was cutting into margins.

Nothing drastic had to change. Just knowing where to look shifted the conversation—and the results. Within two quarters, cash flow stabilized, and decision-making started to feel grounded again.

Financial Reports Are Clues—If You Know What to Look For

Too many CEOs treat financial reports as something to avoid—or something to agonize over when the business feels off. But your reports are more than history—they're diagnostic tools.

These reports won't tell you everything. But used the right way, they help you spot problems early and prioritize where to act. They'll reveal patterns—like expenses creeping up faster than revenue, or invoices piling up without a clear collection plan.

The goal isn't perfection. It's pattern recognition. Once you know what's normal, you'll know when something's off. That's the difference between flying blind and leading with confidence.

If you're checking reports but still feel unclear about what to do next, the problem isn't your spreadsheet—it's the lack of connection between your numbers and your systems.

Let's say you see profits shrinking. Instead of asking, "How do I cut costs?", ask, "Which system isn't holding up?" Is your team reworking projects too often? Is delivery dragging past what was scoped? Is your pricing off?

That shift—from staring at numbers to solving business problems—is where financial visibility becomes a leadership advantage. You're not trying to become an accountant. You're trying to lead a business that actually works.

The sooner you connect the dots between your numbers and their root causes, the sooner you can stop reacting and start leading.

You don't need a CFO to gain financial visibility. But you do need clean, current books and regular reviews. Whether you've got an in-house team or a trusted bookkeeper, someone needs to keep your records accurate and up to date. And you need access to three basic reports: your income statement, balance sheet, and cash flow statement.

With these reports in hand, you can move from guessing to diagnosing. So let's look at seven places where cash tends to get stuck—and what that tells you about the systems behind it.

The 7 Places Cash Hides—and How to Find It

By now, it should be clear that financial stress doesn't always mean you need to "make more money." Often—especially when a business is growing broke—it's already generating enough revenue. But somewhere along the way, the cash gets stuck. More often than not, the clues are already in your financial reports. You just need to know how to read them and what they're really pointing to.

"Most financial issues are broken systems showing up on your P&L."

In this section, we'll walk through seven common places where cash hides. These aren't just accounting categories—they're **operational clues**. Each one points to a system that's strained, inconsistent, or out of sync. Once you know how to spot the signs, you can decide what to fix, where to adjust, and how to free up the cash you didn't know was there.

1. Sales to Asset Ratio—Are Your Assets Pulling Their Weight?

What to Know

Sales to Asset Ratio = Sales/Total Assets

This ratio tells you how much revenue your business generates for every dollar of assets you own—things like equipment, software, or even your office lease. A low ratio could mean underused equipment or excess capacity that isn't generating enough return on the investment.

For example, if your sales in a given period are $750,000 and your assets are valued at $250,000, your sales-to-asset ratio is 3:1. That means you're generating $3 in revenue for every $1 invested in assets.

Why Cash Gets Stuck Here

You may be paying to maintain tools, technology, or space that aren't actively contributing to revenue. Or you may have the capacity to take on more work without adding more infrastructure, but haven't optimized around that yet.

Is This a Problem Area?

- ☐ Are you consistently investing in new tools or equipment without seeing a clear return?
- ☐ Do you have idle space, unused licenses, or underbooked staff or gear?
- ☐ Could you serve more clients with what you already have?

If yes: Evaluate whether your asset purchases align with actual revenue growth and whether your team is structured to maximize what you already have.

> **Rule:** The only reason to buy an asset is to generate revenue and income.

2. Gross Profit—Are You Losing Cash Every Time You Deliver?

What to Know

> Gross Profit = Sales - Cost of Goods Sold (COGS)

Gross profit is what's left after subtracting the cost of goods sold. For product-based businesses, COGS includes the cost of materials and supplies, contract labor, delivery-related tools, and packaging and shipping—everything directly tied to fulfilling an order. For example, a florist's COGS would include flowers and vases. In service-based businesses, unless you use contractors to fulfill specific work, your COGS may be zero.

Gross profit is a key indicator of how efficiently you deliver. (Note: This does not include operating expenses, which are part of net profit.)

Why Cash Gets Stuck Here
Even with strong sales, underpricing, less-than-ideal pricing of materials and supplies, or inefficient delivery eat away at your gross profit. You're bringing in revenue, but you're spending too much to keep it.

Is This a Problem Area?

- ☐ Are client projects regularly going over budget?
- ☐ Are you discounting just to close deals, without a plan to recover margin?
- ☐ Are you overpaying for materials and supplies or contract labor?

If yes: Reevaluate how you scope projects, price your offers, and negotiate with vendors.

> **Insight:** Gross profit is the only place you get cash to spend or convert to profit.

3. Operating Expenses—Spending Smart or Just Spending?

What to Know

Operating expenses are the everyday costs of running your business—things like salaries, subscriptions, and tools. These are expenses you pay whether you're making sales or not. (Note: Operating expenses are different from your COGS, which vary based on how much you sell.)

Why Cash Gets Stuck Here

As the business grows, expenses tend to creep in—especially if you're adding tools or team members reactively instead of strategically. You might be spending money in ways that aren't actually supporting your gross profit.

Decision Quadrant

Ask these two questions for any expense:

1. Does the current cash flow support it?
2. Does the expense align with today's priorities?

Essential vs. Extra

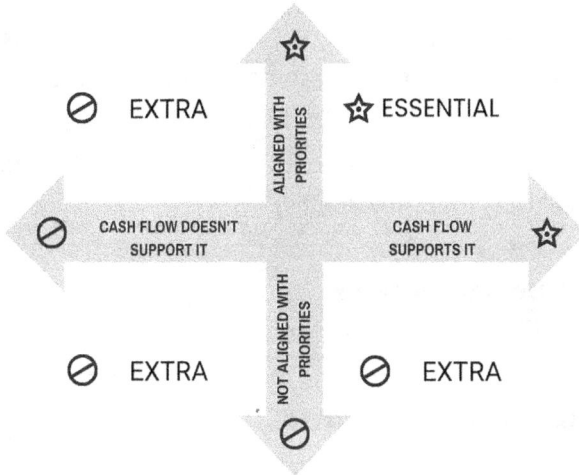

If the answer isn't **yes to both**, it's not essential and should be cut.

Is This a Problem Area?

- ☐ Have you added tools or roles without re-evaluating the return on investment (ROI)?
- ☐ Is there a disconnect between the budget and actual business performance?
- ☐ Is your team trained just to get approval for spending rather than to spend intentionally?

If yes: Use the quadrant as a regular decision-making tool with your team—not just a one-time cleanup.

> **Rule:** For every dollar your gross profit drops, your expenses should drop by a dollar too.

4. Inventory—Is Your Cash Sitting on a Shelf?

What to Know

Inventory includes physical materials or products you've paid for but haven't sold yet. Some accountants split hairs over whether service-based businesses have inventory, but to keep things simple, we'll say that they don't.

Why Cash Gets Stuck Here

Inventory is cash you've already spent—but haven't yet recovered. If it's sitting unused or moving slowly, that money is stuck and unavailable for more urgent needs.

Is This a Problem Area?

☐ Are you reordering products or supplies without reviewing usage rates?
☐ Are there items that haven't moved in weeks or months?
☐ Could you deliver the same value with less inventory on hand?

If yes: Sell slow-moving stock—and **don't reorder** unless it's actively needed.

> **Insight:** Inventory may be an asset on paper, but if it's not moving, it's a cash trap.

5. Accounts Receivable—Is Your Cash Stuck in Unpaid Invoices?

What to Know

Accounts receivable (AR) is money you've already earned but haven't been paid yet. You've sent the invoice, but the cash still isn't in the bank.

Why Cash Gets Stuck Here

Late or inconsistent collections quietly strain your ability to meet obligations. You might be cash-poor, not because you didn't earn it, but because your payment systems are weak or slow.

Is This a Problem Area?

- ☐ Are your payment terms unclear, inconsistent, or unenforced?
- ☐ Do invoices go out late or sit uncollected for weeks?
- ☐ Are your payment options limited or inconvenient for clients?

If yes: Strengthen your AR systems. Use automated reminders, assign someone to follow up regularly, make payment easy for clients, and don't over-accommodate clients at the expense of your cash flow.

> **Insight:** You can't spend what you haven't collected.

6. Accounts Payable—Paying Too Fast and Feeling the Squeeze?

What to Know

Accounts payable (AP) is what *you* owe to others—like vendors and contractors. It's not bad debt, but the timing matters.

Why Cash Gets Stuck Here

Paying bills too fast can tie up cash you could use more strategically. But paying too slow can hurt vendor relationships.

Is This a Problem Area?

- ☐ Are you paying invoices immediately, even when terms allow more time?
- ☐ Are you manually processing every bill, instead of using scheduled or automated payments?

If yes: Align payment timing with your cash flow, not just convenience. Stick to industry norms unless there's a strategic reason not to.

> **Insight:** You don't get bonus points for paying early. Use your terms strategically—especially when cash is tight.

7. Mismatched Financing—Short-Term Debt, Long-Term Regret?

What to Know

Mismatched financing happens when you use short-term funds—like credit cards or lines of credit—to pay for long-term assets, like equipment or office buildouts.

Why Cash Gets Stuck Here

When you use short-term financing, which typically has higher interest rates, to pay for something over several years, interest adds up quickly—and the purchase ends up costing more than expected.

Is This a Problem Area?

- ☐ Are you using credit cards or lines of credit to fund major purchases?
- ☐ Have you broken up a large investment across multiple credit cards just to make it work in the moment?

If yes: Talk to your banker or advisor about refinancing or restructuring your debt. Long-term assets need long-term financing.

> **Rule:** The length of the loan should match the life of the asset.

Now that you've spotted where cash is hiding, the next step is connecting these leaks to the systems behind them. Each spot didn't just reveal a number—it revealed where your operations might be holding you back. Because the real problem isn't just financial—it's structural.

Follow the Cash—Fix the System

Each leak—whether in pricing, receivables, inventory, or expenses—isn't just a cash flow problem. It's a signal. It shows you where the business isn't holding together as it grows.

One of the hardest parts of systematizing is knowing where to begin. But finding hidden cash gives you a built-in roadmap. Instead of guessing, you can prioritize based on impact and fix the part of your business doing the most damage.

"Finding hidden cash is more than a financial exercise. It's a systems audit in disguise."

The good news? You don't need to fix everything at once. But you do need to connect the numbers to what's happening operationally, because the fastest way to improve cash flow is to fix the system behind it.

That's what makes this process so powerful. It doesn't just find the money—it tells you exactly where your foundation needs to get stronger.

In the next chapter, we'll shift from diagnosis to direction. You'll get practical tools to decide which system to fix first, how to break it down, and how to finally get it out of your head—and off your plate.

Because the goal isn't just to find hidden cash—it's to build a business that doesn't lose it in the first place.

Start Smart, Scale Smarter

You don't need to fix it all—just start.
Small, smart moves will do their part.
Pick one pain that slows you down,
And build the system that turns it around.

If it doesn't move the needle, it's just noise.
Pursue a goal that brings sustainable joy.
Structure protects your time and team—
It fuels momentum and powers your dream.

CHAPTER 6

Start Smart, Scale Smarter

"Would you tell me, please,
which way I ought to go from here?"
"That depends a good deal on where you want to get to,"
said the Cat.
"I don't much care where—" said Alice.
"Then it doesn't matter which way you go," said the Cat.
— Lewis Carroll, Alice's Adventures in Wonderland

Before you can scale smarter, you need to know what you're scaling toward—and how to get there without burning out your team, your finances, or yourself.

This chapter helps you do just that. You'll define your overall destination, calculate what your business needs to produce to get you there, and turn that into actionable, focused priorities.

It's not about chasing a random revenue number or trying to fix everything at once. It's about clear goals, high-leverage actions, and building a business that supports your future—one strategic step at a time.

Start with the End in Mind—Then Do the Math

Before you start documenting systems or chasing new revenue, you need to know what you're actually building toward. Without a target, even the best business decisions can lead you in the wrong direction.

Know the Number that Matters

"$1.5 million in revenue."
"$100,000 in profit."

They sound impressive—but are they the numbers that actually matter for your business and your life?

If you've ever set a goal based on what looks good, what others are doing, or what sounds like a nice round figure, you're not alone. But if you're building a business to fund your future—not just fuel growth—you need to define what "enough" really looks like—and why.

"Don't scale toward someone else's finish line."

That's where the concept of transferable value comes in. It's not about revenue. It's not even about what your business might sell for someday. It's about how much the business needs to produce to support the life you want—based on real numbers, not guesses.

Use Transferable Value to Set the Target

Here's where most business owners go wrong—they build the business assuming the sale of the business at the end will make up for all the profit they didn't take out along the way.

But that's a risky bet because you don't control the market, the timing, or the buyer.

A smarter strategy? Build a business that pays you as you go. Design it to produce a steady owner profit that moves you closer to your goal each year. If you sell it later? Great—that's gravy. But your freedom and financial security won't depend on it.

So how do you figure out what your business needs to produce to reach your long-term goal? That's where transferable value comes in—not as a theory, but as a tool. It gives you a clear, practical way to define your target based on what you actually want the business to make possible. It doesn't matter what you want to do with the money—retire, buy another company, expand—but you need to know how much you'll need to transfer from the business to reach your goal.

The Transferable Value Formula

Let's say your goal includes retiring in 20 years, helping your kids pay off student loans, and buying a condo in Florida. After running some numbers, you estimate you'll need $100,000 per year to fund the lifestyle you want after retirement. Multiply that by 25 years (the average length of retirement), and your target becomes $2.5 million.

You've already saved $125,000, which brings the gap down to $2.375 million. That's your transferable value goal, or in other words, the amount your business needs to generate over time to fund your future based on your actual life and financial plans.

Life Goal: Retire in 20 years

$ Needed in Retirement: $100,000 / year

 # Years in Retirement: 25

$ Goal: $100,000 x 25 = $2.5 M

Amount Saved So Far: $125,000

Transferable Value: $2.5 M - $125 K = $2.375 M

Once you've set the number, every strategic decision gets sharper. You're not scaling for the sake of growth anymore. You're scaling with purpose—choosing systems and priorities that move you toward your goal without burning out your team or draining your time.

Turn Your Big Goal into a Monthly Plan

Here's the part that most owners skip—but where all the clarity lives.

Notice in the calculation above, we didn't do anything with the number of years you plan on working until you retire. Now we're going to use it. We're going to take your $2.375 million gap and divide it by how many years you have left before retirement—in this case, 20 years. That's $118,750 per year that you'll need to set aside from the business.

Break it down further, and that's about $9,896 per month. Suddenly, your "someday" goal becomes a concrete monthly target.

Life Goal: Retire in 20 years

Transferable Value: $2.5 M - $125 K = $2.375 M

Annual $ Goal: $2.375 M / 20 = $118,750 / year

Monthly $ Goal: $118,750 / 12 = $9,896 / month

From Monthly Goals to Weekly Focus

If that number feels out of reach right now, that's not a failure—that's a plan. Now you've got something to work toward—and something you can align your team, decisions, and systems around. And when your team knows what success looks like, it's easier for everyone to stay focused, make better decisions, and move in the same direction.

That's the difference between reacting to financial stress and building a business that serves you.

Now that you know your target, the next step is choosing where to focus first. You don't need to overhaul everything—you just need one smart move to start shifting things in the right direction.

How to Spot a Good First Move

Once you know what your business needs to produce, the next question is how you're going to get there. The fastest way to stall out is to try fixing everything at once. The smartest move? Choose one priority that creates real momentum and builds from there.

Start with What Matters Most

There's no shortage of places to start—but not all problems are equally urgent or equally valuable to solve.

"Things which matter most must never be at the mercy of things which matter least." ~ Johann Wolfgang von Goethe

---

Instead of reacting to every fire, look for the one area that would ease the most pressure or unlock the biggest opportunity. If something keeps you up at night or drains your energy week after week, that's your signal. The goal isn't to find the "perfect" fix. It's to pick a meaningful one and move forward.

Find the Pressure Points

In Chapter 5, you learned where cash might be hiding. That wasn't just about stopping leaks—it was about finding leverage.

Pressure points often show up in:

- Accounts receivable that lag for weeks
- Cost of goods sold that eats into your profits
- High operating expenses

- Inventory that ties up too much cash
- Pricing that hasn't kept up with reality

Choosing one of these areas as a starting point doesn't just improve cash flow—it begins changing how the business operates. Because when you fix the system that caused the leak, you're not just putting out a fire—you're preventing the next one. Financial improvements that aren't rooted in operational clarity won't last. That's why the two go hand in hand.

Problems don't live in isolation, and neither do solutions. Fixing one thing often reveals what's broken elsewhere—or makes it easier to solve the next challenge.

Clients First

If your financial leaks and your operational breakdowns *feel* equally urgent, start where they affect your clients.

Systems that touch clients—like delivery, onboarding, invoicing, or support—deserve early attention. Not only do they drive revenue—they also shape your reputation and improve (or at least maintain) client retention. In other words, they're too important to leave messy.

> **Bonus:** Fixing client-facing systems often improves the experience for your team. When the client experience improves, internal handoffs usually do too.

Start the Domino Effect

You don't need a detailed roadmap—just a starting point that moves other pieces with it. Something small enough to act on, but powerful enough to set other parts of the business in motion.

Find the one move that—like a domino—sets off a chain reaction and gets everything else moving. Problems—and progress—rarely stay in one lane. One small improvement often clears the way for the next, or reveals what's been holding everything else back. One that's in the right place can reduce stress, speed up collaboration, and prevent a dozen downstream issues.

"What's the one thing I can do, such that by doing it, everything else will be easier or unnecessary?"

~Gary Keller

Look for improvements that:

- Solve more than one problem at a time
- Free up your time or your team's energy
- Unlock revenue that can't be collected
- Simplify what's gotten too complex

Quick-Start System Prioritization Matrix

Not sure where to begin? This quick-start matrix can help. It highlights common signs that a system is ready for attention and why fixing it matters.

Quick-Start System Prioritization Matrix

Quick-Start Clues	Why It Matters	Examples
Client-touching	Improves experience, retention, and reputation	Onboarding, delivery, invoicing
Frequent/Repetitive	Easier to document, quick time savings	Weekly reports, scheduling, emails
Team Eye-roll	Eases frustration, improves morale	Time tracking, data entry, checklists
Cash Impact	Unlocks hidden cash, improves cash flow	Accounts receivable, cost of goods sold, inventory control
Quick Win/ Low Complexity	Boosts momentum and buy-in	Project management templates, checklists
Big Bottleneck	Reduces chaos, increase capacity	Client handoffs, project kickoff
Strategic Priority	Ties to your monthly or long-term business goals	Proposal process, hiring workflow

Pro Tip: If a system checks two or more boxes, it's ready for attention. Start there.

How One Small Fix Created Big Results

Taylor, CEO of a growing service firm, started by reducing invoice delays. They realized invoices were delayed because the handoff between delivery and admin wasn't clearly defined. So they created a simple checklist and added a five-minute wrap-up step to every project. That one fix sped up cash flow, cut follow-up emails, and freed the team to take on more profitable work. No new hires. No big overhaul. Just one smart move—and the rest followed.

Progress doesn't mean solving everything overnight. It means choosing one high-leverage step and following it through. Next, you'll learn how to do just that, without getting overwhelmed, overcommitted, or pulled off course.

Synergy, Not Silos

Once you've chosen your first move, it's tempting to treat it like a one-off fix. But in most businesses, no issue stands alone. Too often, CEOs solve a problem in isolation without realizing it's connected to five others across the business. Systems don't live in silos—and neither do the problems inside them.

That's why your solutions—and your strategy—must connect across the business.

Sustainable growth starts with alignment. The more your priorities, processes, and people are working toward the same goal, the faster you eliminate friction—and the fewer fires you'll have to put out later.

Alignment is Leverage

You don't need more complexity. You need simplicity, consistency, and decisions that reinforce one another. That's how you protect your progress—and build a business that holds up under pressure.

Scaling isn't about doing more. It means doing better—with intention.

Start by making sure your first goal isn't just a quick fix. It should tie into the bigger picture: your financial target, team capacity, client experience, and long-term goals. That's how you multiply progress instead of piling on pressure.

It's easy to assume the answer is a new tool, a better system, or one more meeting. But more complexity rarely solves the problem. The best solutions are often the simplest—streamlined, focused actions done well and consistently.

The goal isn't constant change. It's building systems lean enough to repeat and strong enough to scale.

Lasting growth comes from repeatability, not reinvention. Growth should feel like momentum, not mayhem. You're not chasing every idea. You're building a business that holds together—when things get busy, when team members leave, even when you step away.

Sustainable scaling is simple, repeatable, team-friendly, and aligned with your goals. With your goals in place and your systems aligned, it's time to sharpen your focus even more.

"Simplicity isn't a shortcut—it's a strategy."

If It's Not Aligned, It's a Distraction

Every opportunity, task, idea, and decision should be measured against your monthly targets and long-term goals. If it doesn't align, it's not a strategy—it's a distraction.

If it doesn't move the needle or reduce the chaos, it's not the next step—it's noise. That doesn't mean ignoring good ideas. It means capturing them for later and staying focused on what moves the business forward.

Alignment is what gives your yes real power—because you're not saying yes to everything. The simpler the goal, the easier it is to stay focused. The clearer the path, the easier it is to bring your team with you.

Grow by Design, Not by Default

Sustainable growth isn't accidental. It's built on clarity, rhythm, and systems that reinforce each other.

Strong systems don't just protect your profit. They protect your time—and help your team do great work without constant check-ins or hand-holding.

That's the shift: from a business built on hustle to one powered by clear, aligned systems.

You don't need a perfect plan to begin. And you don't need to scale every part of your business at once. You need to scale the right things, in the right order, for the right reasons—one aligned step at a time.

If you're like most overwhelmed CEOs, you've tried to do everything at once for far too long. It's time to focus on what really moves the business forward.

You've set your goals and picked your starting point. Now, it's time to make sure the results don't fall apart the minute you step away.

You're not just building a business. You're building a better future—without burning out to get there.

In the next chapter, we'll walk through the 5D Systematization Process—a flexible framework for capturing what works and building systems that support consistent, sustainable growth.

From Chaos to Clarity

The team does it a hundred ways—
It changes slightly every day.
Without a system, nothing sticks—
Just scattered notes and meaningless clicks.

Get it down—then (later) get it right.
Decide, Document, Deploy with might.
Dry Run, Define, then make it real—
That's how true freedom starts to feel.

CHAPTER 7

From Chaos to Clarity — The 5D Process That Makes It Happen

"Start where you are. Use what you have.
Do what you can."
— Arthur Ashe

You've set the goals. You've identified what needs to change. Now it's time to start building systems that get you there—without burying you or burning out your team.

Systematization is what transforms a fragile business into a scalable one—but only if it's simple, sustainable, and clear enough to use when things get busy. You don't need to fix everything at once. And you definitely don't need to do it all yourself. You just need to start.

"You don't have to be great to start, but you have to start to be great." ~ Zig Ziglar

Start with one system. One process. One win. That first documented process becomes the foundation that shows your team what "good" looks like, builds clarity and consistency, and frees you from being the only one who knows how things work. Once you've documented a single process—and watched it save time, reduce questions, or improve delivery—you start to believe. So does your team. And that belief turns into buy-in. That's when real momentum begins.

In this chapter, you'll learn a straightforward method for getting processes out of your head—or out of your team's—and into documented systems that work without overcomplicating the process. Whether you're tightening up an existing process or building something brand new, you'll walk away with a flexible framework that grows with you—no six-figure software stack required.

Systematizing Is Your Responsibility, But It's NOT Your Job

Systematizing is absolutely your responsibility—but it shouldn't be your side hustle. If you try to do all the documentation yourself, it won't get done—or it'll get buried under urgent tasks. The key is to lead the work without getting stuck in it.

Lead the Work—Don't Do the Work

You're the CEO, not the systems documentarian. You don't have to be the one filling out step-by-step guides and formatting checklists. But you *do* have to create the environment where that work gets done—and done well.

The biggest trap CEOs fall into is thinking, "I'll just do it myself—it'll be faster." But systematizing isn't a one-time task. It's a business capability. Building that capability means someone else *owns the how* while you stay focused on the why and what.

Tap or Bring On a Process Integration Lead

It isn't just about asking your most organized team member to "handle systems" in their spare time. You need someone with dedicated time, clarity, and authority to lead the charge. We call this person your **Process Integration Lead**.

They don't need to be a process wizard on day one—but they do need to be coachable, curious, and committed. They'll drive documentation forward, coordinate input from across the team, and make sure your systems don't gather dust in a forgotten folder.

They're also your systems translator and internal project lead. They'll help roll things out in stages, support adoption, and adjust based on team feedback—so the changes stick and survive beyond the kickoff meeting.

Think of them as the architect reinforcing your foundation before growth adds more weight to it.

What Makes a Great Process Integration Lead?

You're not looking for a unicorn. You're looking for someone with the mindset to make things happen.

- **Curious** – Loves asking, "Why do we do it that way?" (and actually listens to the answer)
- **Coachable** – Open to feedback and always game to try a better way
- **Respected** – Trusted by the team and not afraid to follow up (nicely but firmly)
- **Organized** – Thinks in checklists, catches details, keeps chaos in check (and probably color-codes their grocery list)
- **Persistent** – Won't let systems fall off the radar just because things got "busy again"

They're not just documenting—they're translating how your business runs into tools your team can actually use.

Create the Conditions for Success

Want your Process Integration Lead to succeed? Set them up for success from Day 1:

Give Them Time

This role can't be squeezed between client work and admin chaos. Make systematization a priority—not a pet project.

Give Them Access

They need visibility into how things really work—and your support to open the right doors.

Give Them Authority

Empower them to hold the team accountable, especially when old habits creep back in.

You're building a business where systems are the norm—not the exception.

With your Process Integration Lead in place and your first system chosen, it's time to move from idea to implementation. This next phase is where clarity becomes consistency, and your systems become usable, trackable, and real. Here is where clarity becomes currency.

The 5D Systematization Process

If you want systems that actually work, you have to start by being clear on what you're already doing. Not what you wish you were doing. Not what the best-in-class version of your business might do someday. Just what's actually happening now—flaws, messiness, workarounds, and all. That's why we don't start with creating new processes or chasing optimization—we start with clarity on what's happening right now.

That's exactly what the 5D Systematization Process is designed to do. It walks you through five practical steps that—together—make your systems more visible, repeatable, and ready to scale.

Here's how it works:

> Step 1: **Decide** What to Work On
> Step 2: **Document** the System
> Step 3: **Dry Run** the System
> Step 4: **Define** the System Metrics
> Step 5: **Deploy** the System

We'll walk through each step and show you how to make your systems usable and ready for scaling, not just documents collecting dust in a binder.

Step 1: Decide What to Work On

You don't need to scale everything at once. You just need to start. And the smartest place to begin is with *one* system that matters—a process you already use (even if inconsistently) that's ready to get out of someone's head and into a form the whole team can follow.

That first system becomes more than a box checked—it becomes a visible win. It proves to your team—and yourself—that systematization doesn't mean stifling creativity or slowing everything down. It means creating clarity. It means making great work repeatable, not reliant on memory, best guesses, late-night Slack messages... or you!

Don't spend hours (or days) agonizing over which system to start with. Just pick one and get moving.

5D Systematization Process

Decide What to Work On

↓

Document the System

↓

Dry Run the System

↓

Define the System Metrics

↓

Deploy the System

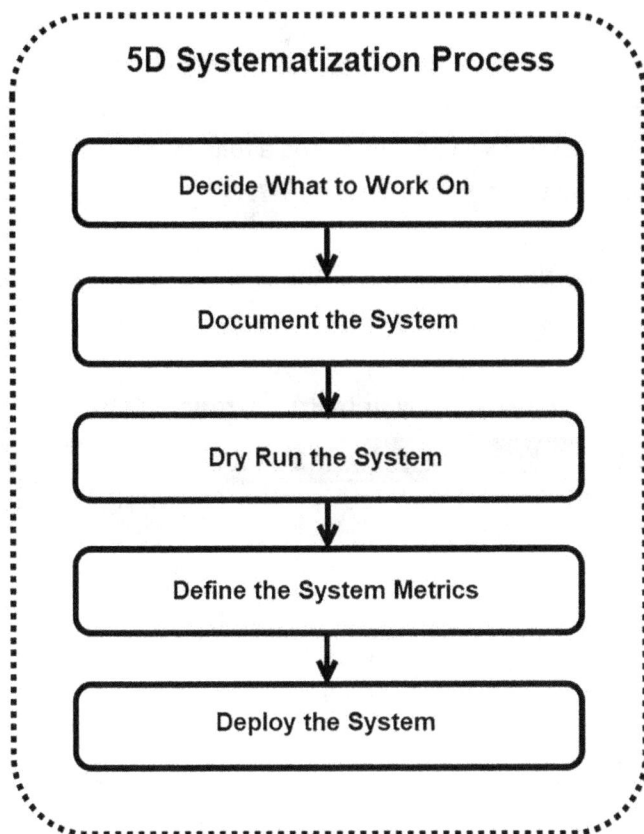

"One System. One Process. One Win."

Chapter 6 gave you the Quick-Start Systems Prioritization Matrix to help decide where to begin. Your first system might directly affect cash flow—like invoicing or getting paid faster. Or it might shape your client experience, like client onboarding. Or maybe it's a task your team rolls their eyes at every week—something simple that somehow still feels chaotic. You might even choose something you do all the time, but never the same way twice.

There's no single "right" system to start with. But there are leverage points—those spots in your business where a small shift creates a high-impact ripple. You don't need a fully mapped strategy. You just need one smart move.

Pick your starting line. Commit. And take the first step that starts changing everything.

Quick-Start System Prioritization Matrix

Quick-Start Clues	Why It Matters	Examples
Client-touching	Improves experience, retention, and reputation	Onboarding, delivery, invoicing
Frequent/Repetitive	Easier to document, quick time savings	Weekly reports, scheduling, emails
Team Eye-roll	Eases frustration, improves morale	Time tracking, data entry, checklists
Cash Impact	Unlocks hidden cash, improves cash flow	Accounts receivable, cost of goods sold, inventory control
Quick Win/ Low Complexity	Boosts momentum and buy-in	Project management templates, checklists
Big Bottleneck	Reduces chaos, increase capacity	Client handoffs, project kickoff
Strategic Priority	Ties to your monthly or long-term business goals	Proposal process, hiring workflow

Pro Tip: Get more bang for your buck by selecting a system that fits into two categories! For example, a process that impacts both cash flow and productivity.

Step 2: Document the System

Documentation is where systematization actually begins. Until it's written down, a process doesn't exist—at least not in a way your team can follow, improve, or depend on. Even a halfway-decent process followed consistently is better than five people doing it five different ways.

"Get it down, then get it right!"

Once a process is documented and in motion, you can begin refining it. But first, you have to capture it—and make it visible enough to be shared, used, and repeated. If you try to optimize a process before documenting it, you're just guessing.

> **Pro Tip:** Modeling your top performers is the best-kept secret to rapid systems development.

Here's how to capture the process:

1. **Clarify the Intended Result**
   Be clear about what the process is supposed to achieve. That clarity keeps the process focused and usable.

2. **Pick Your Star Performer**
   Choose the person who handles this task best. If multiple people do it, model the one who gets the best results with the least drama.

3. **Record the Process**
   Decide how you'll record the task—video, screen recording, or a live walkthrough. Then record the task while it's being done. This step is a two-person job: one person does the task while the other (often your Process Integration Lead) captures the steps in real time.

4. **Transcribe and Clean It Up**
   Turn the recording into a clean, numbered, step-by-step document. Keep it clear and simple. Stick to what matters. Avoid messy first drafts or a Frankensteined version made by committee. Ask: Could someone else follow this and get the intended result?

Tips for Simple Documentation

- **Include the basics:** Name of the process, who it's for, the intended result, and clear numbered steps.
- **Keep it simple:** Define any company-specific terms. Use just enough detail to get consistent results.
- **Stay consistent:** Use consistent formatting and plain language. Keep it easy to follow.

---

*"Complexity is the enemy of systematization—
keep it simple."*

No Fancy Flowcharts Required

At this point, someone on your team might be thinking, "Shouldn't we make a flowchart?"

Here's your official permission to skip it.

Flowcharts can be useful later—but they're not the place to start. Most people don't know how to build them properly, and even fewer know how to read them. The time you'd spend fussing with shapes and arrows is better spent documenting more processes.

If the steps are clear, numbered, and easy to follow, you're already winning. Keep it simple. Keep it usable. Move on.

Step 3: Dry Run the System

Now that the process is documented, test the draft, not the process itself (that comes later). You're simply checking whether the documentation is clear, complete, and usable.

Have someone other than the original performer walk through the instructions exactly as written. That surfaces any missing steps, confusing instructions, or assumptions that only made sense in the moment.

If a team member can't follow the steps without asking questions, it's not ready yet.

Incorporate the feedback, then save the revised version where your team can easily find it—not buried in someone's inbox or a mystery folder.

You can also use the recording as a low-effort training resource. If you recorded a video during documentation, new team members can watch the task in action while following the written steps—no 1:1 hand-holding required.

To capture feedback, have the Process Integration Lead observe the team member as they follow the documentation, noting any missing details and confusing steps.

Step 4: Define Metrics

Once a process is documented and in use, you need a way to track whether it's doing what it's supposed to do. That's where metrics come in.

You're not building a dashboard or reinventing your reporting structure here—just pick one to three simple indicators that show whether the process is working as intended. The goal is to bring focus and give your team a way to track performance over time without guesswork.

For example, in a client onboarding process, you might track client satisfaction survey results. For invoicing, it could be days outstanding or the number of invoices sent on time. Only track metrics you'll act on—don't measure things just to fill a dashboard. They need to be meaningful!

Tracking things like "Slack messages sent" or "meetings held" might *look* measurable, but they don't tell you whether work is getting done better, faster, or more accurately. Even "tasks marked complete" in your project management tool can be misleading if there's no quality or outcome attached. Metrics like these are just noise.

You'll go deeper into metrics and ongoing improvement in Chapter 8 where we introduce the AIM Loop.

Step 5: Deploy the System

If it just sits in a folder, a documented process helps no one.

Deployment means putting the system into action—assigning ownership, making it accessible, training your team, and setting the expectation that *this is how we do it here.*

Loop in your Process Integration Lead to guide the rollout. Use the documentation—and video, if available—to train others. Make it clear who owns the process and when it should be used.

Frame the benefits to your team: less confusion, fewer do-overs, more time to focus on what matters. And expect a little pushback—because even good change comes with friction.

If someone resists, it's a performance issue—not a personal preference. Most team members will adapt quickly, especially if they helped shape the system in the first place. People support what they help create.

> **Resistance is (not) Futile.**
>
> Even the best system can hit a speed bump—usually someone who just doesn't want to follow it.
>
> Here's the bottom line: following systems isn't optional. That doesn't mean you ignore feedback—but it does mean the conversation shifts from "Do I have to?" to "How can we make this work?"

> If someone flat-out refuses, treat it as a performance issue. Don't let one person slow down progress for the whole team.

Most resistance isn't about the system—it's about how the change was introduced. Keep communication open. Involve your team early. And make it clear how the system helps them win as well.

No Process? No Problem.

You've seen how the 5D Systematization Process works for documenting systems that already exist.

But what if a process doesn't exist at all?

Good news: new systems can go through the same 5D Systematization steps. You'll just need to start a little differently—with a clear outcome and a rough first draft of steps. From there, you'll walk through the process, just like you would with an existing system.

And chances are, you're already doing some version of that process—you just haven't written it down yet.

That's your opening. Don't wait for perfect—just build something usable.

Start Smart, Even If It's New

Start with the outcome.
Before you map any steps, define what "done well" looks like. That outcome becomes your anchor—it shapes what needs to happen and who's involved.

Build light. Test fast. Improve as you go.
You don't need a polished version on Day 1. Draft the steps, try them out, and revise based on what actually works. Treat it like a prototype—not a final product.

Don't let perfection get in the way of progress.
You're not being graded—you're building. The goal isn't to get it right the first time. It's to create a usable starting point that your team can improve over time. A rough draft in motion beats a flawless plan no one follows.

Build the Habit—Not Just the System

The goal of systematization isn't just to document things. It's to build a business that runs smoothly, scales sustainably, and doesn't depend on you to hold it all together. Every process you systematize makes space for smarter growth.

Make It a Habit, Not a Handoff

It'll feel clunky at first. That's normal. Every time you document and delegate a task, you reinforce a systems-first mindset. You're building a culture where clarity, consistency, and continuous improvement aren't buzzwords—they're just how you operate.

Work the Process at Your Pace

Start small. Work through the 5D Systematization Process with your Process Integration Lead and a few star performers. If you've got the bandwidth, you can eventually run it in parallel across multiple teams. But if not? One process at a time is perfectly fine. The business still has to run, and sometimes, you really do have to slow down to speed up.

Start with client-facing processes, then move into internal functions like finance, HR, or hiring—or use the Quick-Start System Prioritization Matrix to guide your next move. Once you've documented what already exists, the gaps will show themselves. And now, you know how to fill them.

This Is What Freedom Looks Like

Systematization isn't the end of flexibility—it's what creates your freedom. You're not just building a business that can scale. You're building one that supports you without wearing you out.

And here's the real win: once a system is in place and used, you'll start to see what's working—and what's not. That clarity fuels the next phase: optimization.

When clarity connects the dots between process and cash flow, you stop growing broke and start growing profits. That's what it means to lead with a systems-first mindset and build a business designed to scale.

That's exactly where we're headed next.

If you want a quick reference, here's a snapshot of the 5D Systematization Process—what each step looks like in action, and what it helps you achieve.

5D Systematization Process Summary		
Step	What You Do	What it Gives You
Decide	Choose one high-leverage process to start with	A focused starting point
Document	Record and transcribe how the task is actually done	A repeatable workflow
Dry Run	Test the documented steps with fresh eyes	Clear, usable instructions
Define	Pick 1–3 simple metrics to track performance	A way to measure effectiveness
Deploy	Assign ownership and roll it out to the team	Consistent adoption and follow-through

The Multiplier Phase

One small fix can clear the way—
A smoother handoff, a lost delay.
You tweak, you test, then track the gain—
And suddenly, there's less to explain.

No fancy tools, no shiny pitch—
Just sharpened flow without a glitch.
Assess. Improve. Then measure true—
Let data guide what you should do.

CHAPTER 8

The Multiplier Phase

"What gets measured gets managed."
— Peter Drucker

Once your systems are up and running, something shifts. The late-night emergencies taper off. Financial fires become fewer and farther between. Your team stops asking the same questions. It's tempting to exhale, check the box, and move on.

But this is where the real opportunity begins.

Documented systems aren't the finish line. They're the foundation. What you've built so far isn't just helping your business survive— it's setting the stage to multiply what works.

This next phase isn't about doing more—it's about getting more from what you've already built. It's where you stop winging it and start refining. It's where the payoff for all that structure starts showing up in clearer financial trends, more confident decisions, and a business that not only runs more smoothly—but grows more sustainably.

And the best part? You don't need a massive overhaul or a fancy automation platform to get there. You just need a smart, repeatable rhythm for making small improvements that drive real results.

That's where the AIM Loop comes in.

The AIM Loop—Your Shortcut to Smarter Systems

The AIM Loop gives you a rhythm for ongoing improvement. Once a system is documented and deployed using the 5D Systematization Process, the next question isn't "Is it perfect?" The next questions are: "Is it working?" and "How well?"

First, You 5D. Then You AIM.

The 5D Systematization Process helps you **document** your systems so your business runs more smoothly and predictably.

The AIM Loop helps you **optimize** those systems—improving clarity, performance, and results over time.

Think of 5D Systematization as building the structure, and the AIM Loop as how you keep strengthening it as your business grows.

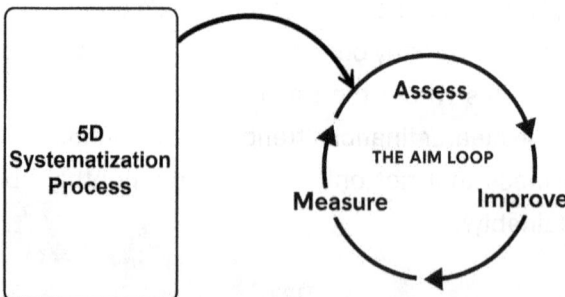

That's the power of the AIM Loop. It helps you answer these questions and make smart refinements without drowning in data, chasing scattered fixes, or overthinking every step. It's about small, focused adjustments that strengthen your systems over time— so they actually deliver the results you need. It's a CEO-friendly rhythm that helps you keep improving without getting lost in data, complexity, or perfectionism.

Here's how you build on the work of the 5D Systematization Process—by transforming a working system into a high-performing one, using both system and financial metrics to make informed, confident decisions.

The result is operational clarity—you're not just guessing where the system stands. You know.

Here's how it works:

> Step 1: **Assess** what's working and what's not
> Step 2: **Improve** the process with small, strategic tweaks
> Step 3: **Measure** the results operationally and financially

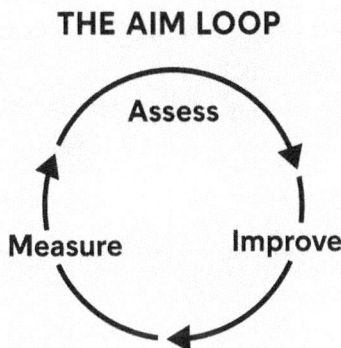

THE AIM LOOP

Assess

Improve

Measure

Each step builds on the last, giving you a practical way to refine and reinforce the systems you've already put in place—so they don't just stay documented, but actually deliver better performance, clarity, and control.

Step 1: Assess

Assess What's Working and What's Not

Before you improve anything, you need to understand what's actually happening—not what you assume, not what should be happening, and definitely not what someone says is happening.

Start by reviewing the operational and financial metrics you defined back in the 5D Systematization Process. Then take an honest look at what the system is producing in real life.

Ask questions like:

- Are the right steps being followed every time?
- Are there delays, rework, or recurring questions?
- Are client handoffs smooth or clunky?
- Are we wasting time waiting for approvals, follow-ups, or missing information?
- Are there repeated mistakes, duplicated effort, or steps that don't add value?
- Are we hitting the outcome this process is supposed to deliver?

You're not trying to analyze every detail or nitpick the team's performance. You're looking for **patterns**—signs that something in the system is creating extra work, costing money, or quietly dragging down results.

Sometimes these issues show up in team feedback—"I'm constantly waiting for X," or "Why does it take three emails to get this step done?" Other times, the clues are financial—shrinking profits, rising delivery costs, or slower turnaround times.

You're not chasing perfection—you're running a systems check. Look at the results, listen to the complaints, and review the data.

Assess what's working and what's not. Patterns tell the truth. Metrics just help you see it faster.

Think of this like a quick inspection of the structure you've built. You're not tearing anything down—you're looking for signs of stress, cracks in the process, or clunky areas. This process gives you the visibility you need to decide what to improve—and what to leave alone.

Not a Data Scientist? You Don't Need to Be.

You don't need to be a spreadsheet ninja or a metrics whiz to use the AIM Loop effectively. You just need to ask better questions—and look at what your system is telling you.

Start by reviewing the 1–3 metrics you identified in the 5D Systematization Process. Are they giving you useful insight? Are they helping you make better decisions?

If one number isn't telling you anything useful, look at a different one. If a question isn't helping you improve the process, ask a different one. The AIM Loop is a system, too. If it's not helping you make better decisions, tweak it until it does.

Step 2: Improve

Improve the process with small, strategic tweaks.

Once you've assessed what's working and what's not, your next move isn't a full overhaul—it's to make **a smart, strategic tweak.**

Find the part of the system that causes the most slowdowns or wasted effort. Then, instead of redesigning everything, ask: "What's one small tweak that could make this system smoother, faster, or easier to follow?"

That small change might look like:

- Adding a checklist or template
- Clarifying a handoff between team members
- Updating a tool or removing one that's not pulling its weight
- Writing a short "how-to" inside your project management tool
- Renaming a shared folder so the team can actually find things

It doesn't have to be complicated—it just needs to reduce confusion, eliminate waste, or improve results.

*"Small improvements done consistently are what **move systems from good to great.**"*

You're not improving the process for the sake of it. You're adjusting the system so it supports the outcome better with fewer dropped balls, fewer workarounds, and less reliance on you to step in when things go sideways.

That's what sets this apart from how most teams approach "process improvement."

Most teams overthink it—or worse, they ignore it until it breaks. You're not doing either. You're building the habit of **refining with intention** before problems become painful.

The Fix Isn't Always Yours to Find

You don't need to come up with every fix yourself.

In fact, your team probably already knows what's not working—they just haven't had a system for speaking up about it. Invite them in. Ask where the process creates friction, feels clunky, or forces them to "just work around it."

You'll get better answers faster when the people who use the system every day help shape how it improves.

People support what they help create.

Step 3: Measure

Measure the results—operationally and financially.

Once you've made a small improvement, you need to know whether it worked—not just felt better, but actually delivered better results.

This step isn't about building a massive tracking system or obsessing over analytics. It's about watching for **meaningful movement** in the places that matter most.

Dashboard Danger Zone

Even the prettiest dashboard in the world won't save a broken system.

Before you build a dashboard, ask:

- Is the system behind this metric working?
- Do I trust the data it's producing?
- Will this chart help me make better decisions?

If the answer is no, hold off.

Dashboards should reflect clarity—not distract from confusion.

Build the system. Test the metrics. Only then automate what matters.

Review the 1–3 metrics you identified in the 5D Systematization Process. These should give you a baseline for how the process was performing before you made the change. Now you're watching for improvement.

Ask questions like:

- Did this change make the process faster?
- Did it reduce confusion or questions from the team?
- Are client handoffs happening more smoothly?
- Are errors or rework happening less often?
- Are we seeing better margins, faster turnaround, or fewer delays?

If you didn't see the result you hoped for, it doesn't mean the tweak was a failure. It just means you've learned something—and you're one loop closer to getting it right.

"Improvement isn't always loud. Sometimes the win is the absence of chaos."

Sometimes the right change shows up in a team's attitude before it shows up in a spreadsheet. And sometimes a tiny tweak unlocks a surprising improvement in cash flow, capacity, or client satisfaction.

When you measure consistently—even at a small scale—you build a feedback loop that strengthens your decision-making and sharpens your leadership instincts. You stop guessing. You start knowing.

Don't Wait for Big Data

You don't need a statistically significant sample—which might be giving you flashbacks to college stats—to decide whether something is working.

If one change saves your team five hours this month... or cuts invoicing errors by half... or gives one client a noticeably better experience—you've already won.

Small improvements add up. And the ability to see them early is what keeps you from abandoning good systems before they have a chance to succeed.

Your job isn't to measure everything. Your job is to measure what matters—and act on what you learn.

Rinse and Repeat

Once you've measured the impact, you're not done—you're just back at the start of the loop.

That's the beauty of the AIM Loop. It's not a one-time fix. It's a habit. A rhythm. A simple way to keep your systems getting better, one small improvement at a time.

Sometimes the next loop shows you something else to improve in the same system.

Sometimes it tells you this one is working well, and it's time to move on.

Either way, you've built the muscle.

You're not guessing. You're learning.
You're not reacting. You're leading.

And that's what makes this system stick.

AIM It, Don't Overthink It

Use this checklist to run your first loop with clarity—not perfection.

- ☐ Choose one system you've already documented
- ☐ Review the system and its financial metrics
- ☐ Ask: What's working—and what's getting in the way?
- ☐ Brainstorm 1–2 small changes to test (clarify a step, add a template, adjust a handoff)
- ☐ Implement and monitor the effect
- ☐ Ask: Did it help? What's the next small move?

Small loops. Big momentum. That's the point.

One Loop. Real Results.
Background:

Riley, the CEO of a software consulting firm, noticed growing tension between her sales and delivery teams.

Projects were getting off to slow, bumpy starts, even though everyone was working hard. Clients were confused about what came next and started following up more often than usual. Timelines were slipping before the work had even begun.

She had already documented the onboarding process using the 5D Systematization Process, but something still wasn't clicking.

AIM in Action

Assess:
Riley reviewed her onboarding metrics: kickoff calls were delayed 60% of the time, and her team reported frequent scope confusion. She spotted the pattern quickly—no one was owning the internal handoff between the signed proposal and kickoff prep.

Improve:
Instead of redesigning the whole process, Riley added a simple 15-minute internal handoff meeting and a quick checklist to confirm deliverables, access, and scope were in place before the project manager was looped in.

Measure:
Within a month, kickoff delays dropped by 40%. Client feedback ratings improved, and the delivery team reported fewer last-minute scrambles. Even sales started surfacing risks earlier because they felt more connected to delivery.

That one win led Riley to run the AIM Loop on her invoicing system next. Each time, she kept it simple: assess one system, make one small fix, measure what matters, and move on.

The right tweak, at the right time, can change everything.

Beyond Optimization—How the AIM Loop Helps You Lead

The AIM Loop was designed to help you improve systems. But once you start using it, you'll discover it gives you something even more powerful—data and visibility.

That visibility doesn't just improve how work gets done—it helps you lead better and scale with intention. Because when your systems produce reliable data, they don't just show you what's wrong. They show you what's possible.

Let's look at two ways CEOs use the AIM Loop beyond pure process improvement.

1. Gain Insight for Smarter Decisions

Sometimes, the process is fine. Nothing's broken. But when you measure, you see something you didn't see before.

That insight can change how you prioritize work, structure your services, or focus your team's energy. It might reveal where your profits are highest—or where you're spending a lot of time for very little return.

Here is leadership intelligence in action—using system-level data to run a smarter business, not just a smoother one.

Example: A consulting firm noticed that their lowest-paying clients required the most handholding, were the least profitable projects, and slowed down other work. The team wasn't doing anything wrong—it was the business model. Instead of redesigning a process, they used the insight to raise prices on high-maintenance clients and improve profitability without changing how the work was done.

> **Pro Tip: Not Every Insight Means a Fix**
>
> If a system isn't broken, don't fix it. But ask what its results are telling you about how your business runs—and how it could run better.

2. Control the Pace of Growth

Growth is a decision, not a runaway train. It doesn't always need to be faster. Sometimes, the smartest move is to slow down—protecting profit, team capacity, or client experience. Remember Rule #4: Slow Down to Speed Up?

The AIM Loop gives you the visibility to do that intentionally.

When you understand how your systems affect profits, workload, and performance, you can scale up—or pause—with purpose. That ability to scale with intention is how you lead by design, not by default.

Using systems data to make those decisions—to speed up or slow down growth on purpose, intentionally and proactively—is the CEO's true superpower.

You choose how fast to go, based on real data and the tradeoffs you're willing to make. No surprises. No emergencies. Just strategy.

Example: A CEO noticed that onboarding was maxing out the team's energy. Rather than push the team harder or hire fast, she used the AIM Loop data to pause new client intake for one quarter. That gave the team breathing room to refine a few key systems—and return with more capacity, less stress, and stronger profit margins.

> **Pro Tip: Slowing Down Isn't Failure—It's Strategy**
>
> There are seasons to push and seasons to pause. The AIM Loop helps you decide—on purpose.

These two ways to use the AIM Loop might look different from system improvements, but the process is the same—**Assess, Improve, Measure.** Whether you're optimizing systems, gaining insight, or managing your pace, the AIM Loop gives you something most CEOs never have:

- Operational clarity
- Leadership intelligence
- Strategic control

And that's exactly what sets you up to lead on purpose—not by accident.

Small Shifts, Big Wins

The AIM Loop isn't about fixing everything. It's about fixing what matters most.

That's how you build momentum—by applying the loop to the 20% of systems that drive 80% of your results. Profitability, client experience, and team workload—these are the areas worth revisiting. Focus your effort where it counts, and momentum will follow.

The beauty of this process is that it scales with you. You don't need a full overhaul. You don't need an automation platform. You just need one good loop at a time.

Fix the Few That Matter

Not every system needs optimizing right away. The ones that touch revenue, delivery, and people? Those are your highest-leverage points.

Go back to the prioritization criteria from Chapter 6—visibility, impact, and team pain points. But now you're not planning at the whiteboard—you're running the loop in real time. Look at which systems are producing the most noise—or have the most potential—and apply the AIM Loop there first.

You're not trying to win everywhere. You're trying to win where it counts.

Build It Low-Tech First

The best improvements don't come from software—they come from clarity.

Add a checklist. Create a template. Rename a folder. Test your fix before you tech your fix—because if it doesn't work manually, it won't work in an app.

High-impact fixes usually don't require a new tool. They require better expectations, smoother handoffs, and fewer workarounds. And if the system starts to hum? That's when you can consider automation—not before.

Templates before tools. Test before you tech. Clarity before complexity.

When to Automate (and When to Wait)

Automation can be powerful—but only if the process works without it. Here's how to know when you're ready:

- ☐ **You've run the process at least 15 times.**
  You've tested it, refined it, and the steps are clear and consistent.
- ☐ **Your team knows what's expected.**
  The system works manually—there are fewer handoffs and less confusion.
- ☐ **You're repeating something often enough to justify it.**
  Automation saves time only if you're doing the task frequently.
- ☐ **You've documented it clearly.**
  You can hand this off and expect consistent results—with or without tech. If those aren't true yet? Start with a checklist or a shared doc.

Tech is a tool—not a shortcut.

Build a Business That Runs Without You

A documented system is useful. An optimized system is better.

But a system that improves itself is priceless.

That's what gives you your time back.

The AIM Loop turns a documented system into a decision-making engine. It doesn't just help your business run better. It helps your business run *without* you.

The more your team can spot issues, test improvements, and track outcomes on their own, the less you have to step in to keep things moving. You're not just building efficiency—you're building independence. The system holds together *even when you're not in the room.*

"Real leadership isn't about control. It's about creating a business that doesn't need it."

That shift—from needing to control everything to building systems that run independently— is how you scale with sanity. Not just more clients, but more control. Not just growth, but growth that doesn't break everything in its path.

And the best part? You don't need to overhaul everything at once.

You just need to keep the loop going—one fix at a time, one insight at a time, one rhythm that never stops improving.

From Optimization to Ownership

Whether you're optimizing systems, gaining insight, or managing your pace, the AIM Loop gives you something most CEOs never have: visibility and control.

But scaling well takes more than solid systems. It takes the wisdom to see your own blind spots—and the discipline to avoid falling into them.

Even smart CEOs with a clear dashboard, a documented process, and a capable team can still hit a wall when momentum turns into missteps.

In Chapter 9, we'll look at what those patterns are—and how to avoid them.

Success Traps that Sabotage Profitable Growth

You meant to help, to lead, to build—
But chaos grows where gaps are filled.
One shortcut here, a silent delay—
And suddenly, you've lost the way.

The habits that once served you well
Now hold you back or hide the tell.
But stop, reflect, and check the map—
There's always a system to bridge the gap.

CHAPTER 9

Nine Success Traps that Sabotage Profitable Growth

"You cannot solve a problem with the same mindset that created it."
— Albert Einstein

Some traps are obvious. Others wear a disguise.

They look like hustle, high standards, flexibility, and loyalty.

They sound like: "I'm just doing what needs to be done."

But underneath, they quietly block momentum, slow progress, and kill profitability—even when it feels like you're doing everything right.

This chapter is about those traps—the ones that keep you in motion but not in control, that make it feel like you're solving problems—but somehow still stuck.

Recognizing these patterns isn't about self-judgment—it's about clarity. When you can spot these traps early, you give yourself the power to course-correct, rebuild stronger, and scale sustainably. Awareness is the first step toward becoming not just the hero of your business—but the architect of its next level.

The first eight chapters gave you the blueprint. This chapter clears the path.

Let's make sure nothing gets in your way.

Good Intentions, Bad Results

Some of the traps that hold you back the most are wrapped in what looks like good leadership.

You're showing up. You're being helpful. You're doing what seems responsible—jumping in when the team is overwhelmed, solving problems quickly, keeping things moving. But doing what seems responsible in the moment often prevents you from leading the way the business really needs.

These first few traps come from a good place. You care deeply about the work, the people, and the future. But if you're always operating from urgency or perfection, there's no space to build the structure that actually gets you there.

Success Trap #1: Endless Action, No Traction

You're moving nonstop. Meetings. Decisions. Fixing broken things before anyone notices. You tell yourself, "It's just a busy season," or "Once we hire the right person, I'll finally have time to focus."

But the season never ends. There's always another fire. Another deadline. Another thing pulling your attention back into the weeds. Here's how you start growing broke: always moving, never building.

The trap of urgent over important shows up when you're doing a lot, but building very little that lasts. That's because most of your energy is going toward symptoms, not systems, and solving the same problems over and over again instead of fixing the root cause.

That's not sustainable. It's also not strategic. Because busy-ness, even when well-intentioned, doesn't equal forward progress.

What This Trap Sounds Like

- "I'll deal with that once things calm down."
- "I'm too busy putting out fires to work on systems."
- "We just need the right person or tool to fix this."

Escaping this trap means making space for the kind of work that doesn't just solve today's problem—it sets the business up to run better tomorrow. When you start focusing on structure instead of speed, things stop slipping through the cracks. You stop reacting and start leading on purpose.

Escape Plan

- Block one hour weekly for systems—treat it like a client meeting you won't skip.
- Pick one recurring fire and ask: "What system would prevent this from happening again?"
- Protect 10% of your week for working on the business—not just in it.

"You don't need more hours—you need a business that works without chasing it."

Success Trap #2: Can't Let It Go

You've delegated here and there—but somehow it all still ends up on your plate. You're holding onto work that should've been offloaded long ago. Sometimes it's because your team isn't quite ready. Sometimes it feels faster to do it yourself. And sometimes you haven't had the time to teach or follow up properly.

This trap convinces you that being in control equals being responsible. But if everything depends on you, your business can't grow—and you can't step away.

You're not protecting quality. You're becoming the bottleneck.

The longer you hold on, the more frustrated your team becomes—they stop stepping up. The systems you built? They collect dust. The business stays fragile because everything still flows through you.

Letting go isn't about giving up control. It's about building systems that create control—without your constant involvement.

What This Trap Sounds Like

- "It's just easier if I do it."
- "They're not ready to take this on yet."
- "I'd delegate it, but I know I'll just have to redo it."

You'll know you've escaped this trap when your team makes decisions without waiting on you, when work moves forward while you're away. When letting go doesn't feel like a risk—it feels like relief.

Escape Plan

- Pick one task you do weekly and hand it off— with clear expectations and a feedback loop.
- Ask yourself: "What's the worst that would happen if I didn't touch this?"
- Turn quality control into a teachable system, not a solo burden.

"Letting go doesn't mean lowering your standards—it means raising your systems to meet them."

Success Trap #3: Trying to Know It All

You feel like you should already have the answers. So instead of asking for help, you stay quiet.

After all, you've built this business. You're the expert. You've gotten this far by being resourceful and figuring things out on your own. And maybe part of you believes that needing help means you're not the kind of leader your business deserves.

But that belief creates its own trap.

When you try to be the expert in everything, you can't focus on the parts that actually need your leadership. And your team stays stuck—because no one is modeling what it looks like to ask questions, share gaps, or bring in outside expertise.

Eventually, this pattern burns you out—and bottlenecks the business. The team hesitates to make decisions. Progress stalls. And the only person who feels fully responsible... is you.

"The smartest leaders surround themselves with even smarter people!"

Escape Plan

You don't have to be the one who knows everything—you just have to be the one who builds a business that doesn't depend on your knowledge alone. Ask for help sooner. Get support where you're stuck. The smartest CEOs aren't the ones with all the answers—they're the ones who know where to get them.

From Scrambling to Scalable

Kendall ran a boutique development firm where everything ran through her—from pricing to proposals to project timelines. She thought she was being efficient, but most of her time was spent putting out fires and redoing work.

She wanted things done right. But instead of building systems or delegating, she kept jumping in herself. Every decision, every deliverable, every issue came back to her.

Eventually, she realized the problem wasn't the team—it was the structure. She started small: a simple handoff checklist, a few SOPs, and weekly check-ins that didn't involve her running the show. She brought in a project manager to run the day-to-day and gave her team more ownership.

They stepped up—and Kendall finally stepped back.

People Avoidance Patterns

Leading people is one of the most rewarding parts of business—but also one of the hardest parts. You care about your team. You want to be fair, kind, and respectful. But that desire can quietly turn into hesitation—avoiding conflict, sidestepping expectations, or withholding feedback because you don't want to rock the boat.

These traps don't look like poor leadership on the surface. In fact, they often stem from trying to be a good leader. But when clarity and accountability go missing, even strong teams lose momentum—and your best people might walk away without ever telling you why.

Success Trap #4: Avoiding the Hard Stuff

You know something's off. A team member is falling short. Expectations aren't being met. Deadlines are slipping. But instead of addressing it directly, you wait. You don't want to micromanage—or make things awkward—or create more drama in an already overloaded week.

This trap convinces you that avoiding conflict is protecting morale. But when you stay quiet, your top performers notice—and over time, they disengage or leave.

It's not just about feedback—it's about clarity, accountability, and culture. When people don't know where the line is—or what happens when it's crossed—standards fade, trust erodes, and your A-players start to wonder if it's worth giving their best.

What This Trap Sounds Like

- "They're trying their best—I don't want to crush them."
- "This isn't the right time to bring it up."
- "They should know that's not acceptable by now."

You'll know you've escaped this trap when your team trusts that you'll say what needs to be said—and do it with respect, when accountability isn't a surprise. And when your culture makes space for growth, not confusion.

Escape Plan

- Schedule a check-in with the team member you've been avoiding—and come in with specifics, not assumptions.
- Clarify expectations and follow through consistently (not just when things fall apart).
- Don't wait for things to escalate. Small, direct conversations now prevent bigger problems later.

Success Trap #5: No One's on the Same Page

You thought you were clear. The team said they understood. But things didn't happen the way you expected—or didn't happen at all.

Projects stall. Priorities shift. Accountability gets fuzzy. And everyone starts blaming "communication issues."

This trap doesn't just show up in how you speak—it shows up in how things are reinforced (or not). Without clear expectations, consistent follow-through, and systems that support execution, people default to doing it their own way—or not at all.

"You don't rise to your goals—you fall to your systems."

What This Trap Sounds Like

- "I thought I was clear."
- "We talked about this already—why wasn't it done?"
- "I didn't know the priority changed."
- "I don't know what's expected anymore."

You escape this trap when your systems speak louder than your Slack messages. When your team doesn't just understand priorities—they act on them. And when you're no longer the only one holding the vision together.

Escape Plan

- Turn verbal instructions into written systems— then share them where the team actually looks.
- Ask your team to repeat back priorities at the end of key meetings (don't assume alignment).
- Tie expectations to deliverables—not just intentions.

From Avoiding to Aligning

Avery had a rockstar team—on paper. But tension was growing. Deadlines were getting missed, one team member kept dropping the ball, and others were picking up the slack without saying a word.

Avery didn't want to seem heavy-handed. She told herself, "They know what's expected—they just need more time." But when her best developer resigned unexpectedly, citing "frustration with lack of clarity," she realized silence was costing her more than she thought.

She sat down with the team, reset expectations, and made accountability part of the culture—not just a response to crisis. Things didn't shift overnight, but the tone changed. The top performers stayed. And the chronic underperformer either stepped up—or stepped out.

Fragile Foundations

Growth without structure always feels heavier than it should.

This next category of traps shows up when your business is running—technically—but not holding together well. You've got systems, but they're outdated, ignored, or duct-taped together. Or you're still relying on memory, heroic effort, and "just figure it out" energy.

That might have worked early on. But now? It's costing you.

These traps highlight what happens when the foundation underneath your team's work is either missing or not strong enough to support your next level of growth. Without a strong foundation, even smart growth leads to growing broke.

Success Trap #6: Process? What Process?

You have systems—or at least you had them. But they're buried, outdated, or skipped when things get busy.

This trap hides in plain sight. You think you've "checked the box" on process. But if your team isn't actually using it, it might as well not exist.

When systems aren't used, followed, or updated, you end up paying twice—once in wasted time, and again in inconsistent results. And you become the fallback answer to every question.

Good processes don't live in documents. They live in behavior. And if you want them to stick, they need to be easy to find, easy to follow, and reinforced over time.

What This Trap Sounds Like
- "We have a process—I think it's in the old Notion doc."
- "We follow it... most of the time."
- "It depends on who's doing it."

You escape this trap when processes are easy to follow and hard to ignore. When you're not the one reminding people to use them. And when quality doesn't dip just because things get busy.

Escape Plan

Don't just document the process—make sure people use it. Bring your team into the process early, and build systems that are simple, visible, and actually followed.

Success Trap #7: Red Flags Don't Fix Themselves

Something's off—a project slipped, a client is quietly unhappy, and a delay is starting to snowball. But instead of addressing it head-on, you brush it aside—it's not urgent yet. You'll deal with it later.

This trap tells you to wait—to hope the issue resolves on its own. But red flags don't disappear. They compound. And by the time it becomes urgent, it's also expensive.

You don't need to micromanage. But you do need to listen when your business is trying to tell you something.

Early action prevents full-blown fire drills, and consistent follow-through signals that you're not just watching metrics— you're using them.

"Small issues left alone become big, expensive ones.
Listen early. Act early."

What This Trap Sounds Like

- "That's not great, but it's a one-off."
- "I'll bring it up next week."
- "I don't want to overreact."

You escape this trap when you stop waiting for problems to escalate—when your team knows small issues get addressed early, and your culture rewards raising concerns—not hiding them.

Escape Plan

- Review recent problems and ask: Did we fix the issue—or just move past it?
- Encourage your team to bring up red flags early—and act when they do.
- Treat small breakdowns as clues, not annoyances.

From Chaos to Consistency

Casey had grown her consulting team fast—but the systems hadn't kept up. Handoffs happened in Slack, deadlines slipped, and clients were starting to notice.

She thought she just needed better time management. But when a key deliverable fell apart, she realized the process itself was the problem.

So she started documenting what already worked: clear checkpoints, simplified task lists, and shared timelines. She looped in her team to co-create the new system and built feedback loops into weekly stand-ups.

It didn't just improve project flow—it surfaced hidden issues before they escalated—and gave Casey a peace of mind she hadn't felt in months.

Financial Blind Spots

You've worked hard to lead your team and tighten your systems. But there's one area most CEOs still avoid until it becomes a problem—the numbers.

Most CEOs don't set out to avoid the financials—but when you're overwhelmed, it's easy to push off what feels complex, unclear, or uncomfortable. You assume that if sales are up, profit will follow—or that if someone else is handling the books, the business must be fine.

But just like people and processes, your numbers need clear ownership and active leadership. These traps aren't about spreadsheets—they're about visibility, responsibility, and profit. And the sooner you face them, the faster you'll stop growing broke—and start growing wisely.

Success Trap #8: Confusing Revenue with Results

Sales are up. The team's busy. But profit hasn't moved. You're working harder than ever—and it's not translating into real financial progress.

You're growing—but you're also growing broke.

This trap tells you that if the top line looks good, everything else will work itself out—but it rarely does.

Revenue is loud. Profit is quiet. And if you're not tracking both, it's easy to chase growth that doesn't actually serve your business.

You don't need to become a financial expert. But you do need to stop treating revenue as the only scoreboard that matters.

> **What This Trap Sounds Like**
> - "We're doing great—our revenue's up 40% this year!"
> - "We just need to sell more."
> - "I'm not sure where the cash is going, but I know we're growing."

Success Trap #9: No One Owns the Numbers

You get financial reports—but you don't look at them regularly. Or you do... but you're not sure what to do with them. Your bookkeeper handles the data. Your team watches top-line revenue. But no one is truly responsible for owning the numbers and using them to steer the business.

This trap is subtle—but dangerous. When no one owns the numbers, they lose meaning. You can't spot red flags or connect performance to outcomes. And eventually, you start making gut decisions your business can't afford to get wrong.

Numbers don't need to be your job—but they do need to be someone's. And they need to mean something to the team—not just to your accountant.

What This Trap Sounds Like

- "I'm not really a numbers person."
- "We look at the finances when we have time."
- "That's the bookkeeper's job, right?"

Finance Clarity Builder

How to escape the most common financial blind spots—and lead with numbers, not just instinct.

If you're confusing revenue with results...	If no one owns the numbers...
Check your margins, not just sales.	Pick one key metric to track weekly.
Price for profit—not just growth.	Review financials with your team—not just your bookkeeper.
Slow down before saying yes to more work.	Make your numbers part of how you lead—not just what you file.

From Growth to Gut Check

Quinn ran a niche SaaS company that had doubled its client base in under a year. Revenue was booming—but cash flow was tight, payroll was stressful, and she couldn't figure out why.

A quick review with her bookkeeper showed the truth: her cost to serve had grown just as fast as her client list. Her margins were shrinking—even though sales were up.

Once she saw the numbers clearly, she stopped chasing every new opportunity and focused on refining her service tiers, re-scoping deliverables, and renegotiating vendor contracts.

Three months later, her revenue had leveled off—but her profit had doubled.

From Trap to Transformation

These traps aren't personal flaws—they're predictable patterns. The more your business grows, the more these friction points show up. They masquerade as good intentions: protect the team, work harder, do it right. But left unchecked, they quietly chip away at clarity, control, and profit.

You don't need to fix them all at once. In fact, the smartest way forward is to pick one, act on it, and rebuild from there. That's how progress happens—one thoughtful move at a time.

Before you move on, take a minute to check in. Are any of these traps quietly costing you?

Are These Traps Costing You Profit?

- You feel like you're always working... but not getting anywhere
- You're the only one who really knows how things should be done
- Your top people are leaving—and you're not sure what went wrong
- Processes exist, but no one actually uses them
- You're making more money—but struggling to see where it's going

If more than one of these feels familiar, flip back through the Escape Plans and choose one place to start. One change is all it takes to get momentum back on your side.

Here's where the AIM Loop comes in. The AIM Loop isn't just a tool for optimizing what's working—it's how you keep traps like these from creeping back in. Assess. Improve. Measure. Over time, this loop becomes your rhythm for leading with clarity, instead of firefighting from overwhelm.

To help you move from insight to action, here's a quick-scan guide summarizing the nine traps, what they look like in real life, and how to escape each one with clarity and control. Use it as a reference, a reset button, or a gut-check whenever you feel stuck.

From Trap to Traction

Trap	What It Looks Like	What to Do Instead
Endless Action, No Traction	Constant motion with little forward progress	Block weekly systems time. Prioritize traction over speed
Can't Let It Go	Holding onto work instead of trusting the team	Delegate fully—with standards, not micro-management
Trying to Know It All	Doing it all alone, staying quiet instead of asking	Ask for help. Focus on leading, not knowing everything
Avoiding the Hard Stuff	Skipping difficult conversations or expectations	Speak up. Set clear, kind standards and follow through
No One's on the Same Page	Inconsistent expectations, frustration, rework	Clarify roles. Align the team on what "done right" means
Process? What Process?	Systems exist—but no one uses them	Build usable processes your team actually follows
Red Flags Don't Fix Themselves	Delayed decisions, overlooked issues	Listen early. Act early. Prevent small issues from growing
Confusing Revenue with Results	High sales, low clarity on profit	Monitor margins. Prioritize profit, not just revenue
No One Owns the Numbers	Financials handled by others, not understood	Own your numbers. Use them to steer, not just report

The good news? When you spot these traps early and take simple, strategic action to escape them, everything changes.

You reclaim your time. You rebuild profit. You lead without carrying the whole business on your back.

That's what Chapter 10 is about: the transformation that happens when you stop growing broke—and start leading the kind of business that works—with or without you in the room.

Your Dream Business (and Life) Awaits

You're no longer holding it all in your hands—
The team runs strong, the systems stand.
Time to think. Space to lead.
Profit that flows without constant speed.

You built with purpose, you scaled with care—
New freedom meets you everywhere.
Not built on chaos. Not built on grind.
But clarity, profit, and peace of mind.

CHAPTER 10

Your Dream Business (and Life) Awaits

"The future depends on what you do today."
— Mahatma Gandhi

You didn't start your business just to survive.

You started it with a vision: doing work that matters, making your own decisions, and building something that reflects your values. You imagined freedom. Control. The flexibility to shape your time around what matters most. And space to show up—not just for your clients and your team, but for yourself and the people you love.

But somewhere along the way, that dream got buried under demands. Sales are coming in, but profit still feels out of reach. You're doing too much—and somehow, it's still not enough. From the outside, it looks like success. But inside, it's wearing you down.

You've been growing—but maybe not in the ways that matter most to you. Maybe it's costing you your time, your energy, or your peace of mind.

This chapter shows you what it looks like on the other side.

What it looks like when the business doesn't just survive—but supports the life you wanted from the start. Your systems carry the weight. Your team shows up strong. And your numbers give you the confidence to say "yes" to what excites you—and "no" to what doesn't in your business and in your life.

Because your dream wasn't just to build a business that grows.

It was to build one that gives back to your life, your values, your future.

Now, you're closer than you think to a life where you wake up without dread. You don't have to check your inbox before breakfast. You know what matters today—and what can wait.

From Overwhelmed to In Control

When you're stuck in the weeds, the work never stops—but progress feels optional. You're juggling decisions, approvals, deliverables, and people. And even though you're putting in long hours, things still slip through the cracks. The business runs on urgency, not intention. No matter how capable you are, you're tired of being the glue holding everything together.

Here's what happens when that changes.

You're Back in the Driver's Seat

At some point, it stopped feeling like you were running the business—and started feeling like it was running you. Your days are dictated by who pings you next, what went wrong this time, and which ball just got dropped. You're reacting all day—and still ending the week with half your priorities untouched.

But with the right systems, you no longer run on panic—or whoever's yelling loudest. You have clarity on where the business is going and what it needs from you to get there. You have a pulse on how things are performing—without hovering. You're no longer the human fail-safe. You're setting the direction.

You're done fighting fires. Now, you're driving the engine.

Space to Think and Time to Lead

Right now, the big ideas are collecting dust at the bottom of your to-do list. You want to be more strategic, but between project reviews, Slack messages, and last-minute "quick questions," there's no white space left. You're stuck in execution mode—and every time you carve out thinking time, it gets swallowed by something urgent.

But when operations stop depending on your constant presence, your calendar opens up—and so does your mind. You get time back—not just for tasks, but for leadership. For strategic decisions. For working on the business—not just in it. And for something even more valuable: presence. With your team, your family, and yourself.

Here's when the role of CEO starts to feel sustainable—and energizing again.

You Know What Moves the Needle

When every decision feels like a guess, you either hesitate—or push forward on instinct, hoping for the best. You're surrounded by information, but not insight. In the back of your mind is that question you can't shake: "Is this even making a difference?"

When your operational systems are tied to financial reality, the guesswork disappears. You know which efforts are producing results—and which are just noise. You can prioritize with confidence because your data tells a story you trust. It's not about tracking everything. It's about focusing on the right things and letting go of the rest.

Clarity isn't just comforting—it's powerful. It lets you lead decisively, instead of chasing what's urgent.

"Here's where clarity becomes currency—giving you the insight to invest your time, energy, and resources where they matter most."

This shift takes you from being buried to being intentional. From having your day pulled out from under you to shaping it with purpose. But control isn't just about your calendar—it's also about your team.

The transformation continues when you're no longer the bottleneck between ideas and execution.

From Bottlenecks to Built-In Trust

When everything flows through you, progress stalls—and stress builds. You're answering questions, double-checking work, rewriting deliverables, and jumping in at the last minute to keep things on track. Not because you want to micromanage, but because you care deeply about the quality of the work and the client experience. Too often, it feels like if you don't catch the details, no one will.

But what if the business didn't rely on your eyes, your edits, or your involvement to maintain your standards?

Here's what it looks like when trust isn't a leap—it's built in.

Everyone Knows What "Done Right" Means

When expectations are vague, everything takes longer. Your team hesitates, second-guesses, or improvises—delivering something that misses the mark—and you end up redoing it under a deadline. It's not a talent issue. It's a clarity issue.

But when your systems define what "done right" looks like, everything shifts. Your team works with more confidence because the standards are clear. The back-and-forth decreases. Quality becomes consistent—not because you checked it, but because the process reinforces it.

You're not lowering your standards to delegate. You're documenting them—and that's what makes them sustainable.

Delegation That Actually Works

Right now, delegation often feels like a gamble. You hand something off, hoping it won't come back needing cleanup—or cause more problems than it solves. Sometimes, it's easier to do it yourself than explain it again.

But with the right structure, delegation stops feeling risky. Ownership is clearly defined. Handoffs are clean. The person responsible knows what success looks like and how to get there.

You're no longer the fallback plan. You're the one creating the conditions for your team to thrive—without hovering or holding their hands.

The benefit isn't just operational. You stop carrying the weight of every detail and deadline. You start breathing easier—not just at work, but after hours too.

Culture That Carries the Business Forward

When you're stretched too thin, your values get applied inconsistently. One team member goes above and beyond while another slips on the basics. Feedback gets skipped. Standards get blurred. Over time, the culture starts to wobble under the pressure.

But when accountability and clarity are built into your systems, culture stops being aspirational and starts becoming operational. Expectations don't just live in your head—they live in the process. That creates alignment at every level.

Now your team isn't just working hard—they're working smart, together, and in the right direction. You're not the only one pushing things forward. You're surrounded by people who own the mission like you do.

This pivotal shift is the moment your team starts moving in sync—with each other and with you. You're no longer the hub of every decision. You've built a system that reinforces your standards, empowers your team, and gives you room to lead.

And the transformation continues when your operations stop depending on duct tape—and finally start running smoothly.

From Chaos to Smooth Sailing

When things are duct-taped together behind the scenes, the cracks eventually surface. Projects get stuck. Deadlines shift. Clients feel the ripple effects even if they can't name them. The business is stuck in reaction mode—responding to the latest issue without the systems to prevent the next one.

Growth doesn't create chaos—it reveals it. If your business is held together by memory, hustle, and good intentions, it will eventually crack under pressure.

What Smooth Systems Really Change

Growth doesn't just create chaos—it exposes it. Here's what it looks like when a fragile business gets reinforced—before it breaks.

Before	After
Every Monday started the same way—five Slack threads blowing up, one client project already behind, and a critical process step only one person knew how to do (and they were out sick).	The team kicks off with a shared dashboard, a clear workflow, and the confidence that every deliverable has a home—and an owner.
No one was slacking—everyone was doing their best. But best efforts without structure meant missed deadlines and burnout.	Processes are documented. Capacity is visible. The CEO still checks in—but doesn't have to rescue.
It felt like treading water—until something broke.	There's a rhythm to the work. Growth doesn't mean more chaos—it means more progress.

This kind of stability isn't luck—it's built. It starts with systems that don't rely on your constant oversight.

Systems Don't Need Babysitting

Right now, most processes live in people's heads—or worse, in scattered documents that no one checks. If someone leaves, things break. If a project goes sideways, you have to step in to get it back on track.

But when your systems are well-documented, clearly owned, and consistently followed by the team, everything runs more smoothly. You can step away without holding your breath. You can onboard new hires without having to recreate your knowledge from scratch. The business stops relying on heroic effort and starts operating with consistency.

With that consistency comes a subtle but powerful shift: you're able to unplug without guilt. Take a vacation without dread. Sleep through the night without worrying about what might fall apart before morning.

Problems Solved!

In reactive mode, small issues snowball fast. By the time you realize something's off, it's already impacting the team, the client, or the bottom line. Instead of solving it, you're slapping on a quick fix—because there's no time to pause and address the root cause.

But when your systems surface red flags early, you don't just react—you resolve. You catch breakdowns before they spiral. You fix what caused the issue, not just the symptoms. Over time, the business becomes more resilient, not more fragile.

Crisis mode ends not because nothing goes wrong—but because you've built a structure that responds quickly and wisely when it does.

Growth Without the Growing Pains

When your systems can't keep up with your growth, success becomes its own source of stress. Every new client stretches the team—every new offer strains delivery. You're stuck choosing between opportunity and burnout, and neither option feels like a win.

Once your systems are scalable, growth stops feeling risky. You don't have to rethink how the business runs every time you level up. You already have the foundation—and now you're just building on it.

Instead of fearing what growth might break, you get to plan for what it will enable. That changes how you lead—and how you live.

That's the power of aligned systems: you stop scrambling and start scaling. The chaos settles. The pressure lifts. And what used to feel fragile now feels solid.

And the transformation continues when your financials stop keeping you up at night—and start giving you peace of mind.

From Growing Broke to Growing Profits

You've put in the work. Clients are coming in. Revenue is up. Yet when you look at your numbers, something doesn't add up. The cash isn't there. The profit margins are thinner than they should be. Despite the growth, it still feels like you're barely keeping up—financially, mentally, and emotionally.

That's what growing broke really looks like. It doesn't have to stay that way.

Cash Flow You Can Count On

Right now, you're tracking payments in spreadsheets, checking the bank balance a little too often, and crossing your fingers that the next client payment clears before payroll hits. You're not in control of the money—you're chasing it.

But when you have systems that align your operations with your financials, everything changes. You see what's coming in, what's going out, and what needs attention—*before* it becomes a crisis. You're no longer waiting for a bookkeeper to confirm what your gut already knows. You know your numbers—and more importantly, you trust them.

That confidence brings something you haven't felt in a long time— peace of mind. It lets you plan, prepare, and decide from a place of strength—not stress.

No More Growing Broke

In a business without strong systems, growth leaks money. You overspend to fix what's broken. You rely on duct tape to deliver. You hire out of desperation. And even as revenue rises, profits decrease.

When you plug those leaks—through clear processes, defined roles, accurate pricing, and smarter decisions—profit stops being a mystery. It becomes predictable. Repeatable. Real.

"You're not just earning more. You're keeping more."

When your operations, people, and financials are connected, you no longer have to choose between serving clients well and staying profitable. You've built a business that does both.

Profits Reflect Your True Value

Maybe you didn't start your business just to make money. But that doesn't mean you shouldn't be compensated for the value you've created. You've carried the risk. You've made the tough calls. You've built something out of nothing. And without you, it wouldn't exist.

Now that the business is stable, profitable, and self-sustaining, the reward is no longer theoretical. You're paying yourself well—and without guilt. Distributions become dependable. Financial freedom becomes possible.

With that comes the ability to take care of the people and priorities that matter most to you—not someday, but now.

That's what happens when your business is built with integrity—across your systems, your finances, and your people. You're no longer stuck growing broke. You're growing on purpose. You're growing profits. You're growing strong.

"It's a business that gives back."

---

12 Signs You're Building Your Dream Business

Rate yourself to see where you're thriving—and where to focus next.

Use this list to check in with yourself.

Rate each item on a scale from 1 to 5—where one means "Not at all true right now," and five means "Absolutely true, consistently."

There's no right score—just clues about where you're thriving and where your systems might still need attention.

Sign	1	2	3	4	5
1. You're running the business—it's no longer running you.	☐	☐	☐	☐	☐
2. You have time to think strategically, not just react.	☐	☐	☐	☐	☐
3. Your team knows the mission and drives results without constant oversight.	☐	☐	☐	☐	☐
4. Systems keep things moving even when you're not in the weeds.	☐	☐	☐	☐	☐
5. Problems get solved at the root—not just duct-taped.	☐	☐	☐	☐	☐
6. Revenue is rising *and* profits are strong.	☐	☐	☐	☐	☐
7. Cash flow is predictable—and growing.	☐	☐	☐	☐	☐
8. You're getting compensated for your real value	☐	☐	☐	☐	☐
9. You can say yes or no—strategically, and without guilt.	☐	☐	☐	☐	☐
10. You're not constantly "on"—you can unplug and trust won't fall apart.	☐	☐	☐	☐	☐
11. You're present in your life again—with more energy and less stress.	☐	☐	☐	☐	☐
12. You feel more in control, more energized, and more optimistic about the future.	☐	☐	☐	☐	☐

Now look at your scores.

Which ones are already strong?

Which ones could use a little focused attention this quarter?

You don't need to tackle everything at once. Just pick one— and build from there.

These wins aren't accidental. They're the result of building with intention, structure, and a smarter way to scale.

You started this business with a dream—not just to grow, but to build something that lasts. Something that gives back more than it takes. Something that creates opportunities, security, and joy—for you, your family, your team, and your clients.

That dream still matters. You're equipped to make it real.

A business that runs smoothly. A team you can trust. Systems that multiply your success. Money that doesn't just flow—it builds.

Your dream business isn't just possible—it's waiting for you to step into it.

From Knowing to Doing

You saw the cracks behind the gloss,
The busy wins that came with loss.
You named the gaps you used to miss,
And glimpsed a better way than this.

But clarity alone won't build what's new—
It takes small steps and follow-through.
One aligned move, one path that shows—
That's how you build what lasts and grows.

CONCLUSION

From Knowing to Doing

---

*"The distance between your dreams and reality
is called action."*

— Unknown

You didn't read this book just to collect ideas.

You picked it up because something's not working—and you're ready for that to change.

Maybe you're tired of putting in so much effort for so little return. Your calendar is packed, but your bank account isn't. You're delivering for clients, supporting your team, and trying to keep everything running—but deep down, you know this pace isn't sustainable. If something doesn't shift soon, you'll burn out—or break something.

Now, you know why it feels that way.

You can see the cracks behind the chaos. You've spotted the patterns. You've realized that growing broke doesn't just happen to struggling businesses—it happens to successful ones that outgrow their systems. It happens when the foundation underneath can't keep up with the weight of growth.

You've done the hard work of getting clear.

Now it's time to take the even more important step forward.

From Insight to Impact

You've seen the systems beneath the chaos.

You've identified the gaps in your cash flow.

You've realized that the problem isn't your team—it's the structure.

You've done the hard work of getting clear—and that's no small feat. Most business owners never slow down long enough to do it. But clarity alone doesn't change anything. It won't fix broken handoffs or missed margins. It won't simplify decision-making or protect your time. It won't build a better business.

Action does.

Clarity Alone Doesn't Change Anything

Insight is powerful—but it's not the same as momentum.

You can name what's broken. You can even imagine a better way forward. But unless something shifts in how the business runs, the outcome stays the same.

Here's where many smart, committed CEOs get stuck. They wait until things calm down. Until they've hired. Until they have more time. But that day rarely comes.

The temptation is always to keep planning. Keep reading. Keep organizing your thoughts. But at some point, you have to decide: am I going to build this—or just think about it?

Clarity gives you direction.

Action moves you forward.

Progress Starts with One Step

You don't need a massive overhaul. You don't need a polished plan. And you definitely don't need to fix everything at once.

You just need to start.

Pick one system. One role to clarify. One handoff to clean up. One financial blind spot to investigate.

Even the smallest change can build momentum—and once you feel that forward motion, everything else gets easier.

> **How do you eat an elephant? One bite at a time!**
> Start small. Start smart. Just start.

So why now? Because waiting has already cost you time.

Why not? You already know what needs to change—and you're more equipped than you think.

That's when insight becomes impact.

Not because you understand the problems, but because you finally do something about them.

Freedom, Profit, and Peace of Mind

You didn't start this business to feel buried. You started it to have more freedom—not just over your schedule, but over your decisions, your income, and the way you show up in your life.

But somewhere along the way, the freedom faded. You got busier. The wins got more expensive. And even when revenue rose, it didn't always translate into peace of mind.

This book wasn't just about finding what's broken. It's about showing you what's possible when you fix it.

Because when you stop growing broke, you start building something entirely different:

- A business that supports your life instead of consuming it
- A team that doesn't need your constant oversight
- Financials that tell you the truth—and help you make the right call
- Systems that hold together even when things get busy or you step away

It isn't a fantasy or some idealized version of business ownership. **It's the future you can build—starting now.**

Built for You—Not Just By You

You don't need to keep holding everything together through sheer will.

That's not sustainable—and it's not why you started this.

The strategies in this book aren't theoretical. They're the foundation for building a business that works for you—not one that collapses the moment you unplug.

That means designing systems that don't need babysitting. Financial processes that give you clarity, not confusion. Roles and responsibilities that are owned by your team—not floating in your head.

You're not just building structure—you're building capacity.
Capacity to lead. To think. To step away when needed.
Capacity to focus on what moves the needle—not just what's on fire.

Systems are what allow your business to run without you as the glue.
Financial clarity is what lets you sleep at night.

And your people? They're the multiplier—but only when your systems support them.

That's how your business becomes sustainable—and enjoyable.

Grow, Sell, or Step Away—On Your Terms

When the right systems support your operations, your team, and your finances, you create options. You're not just reacting to what the business demands—you're shaping what it becomes.

Imagine knowing exactly how money is flowing through the business—and what's draining it.
Imagine reclaiming your calendar.
Imagine leading without having to hover.

You're not chasing growth anymore. **You're choosing it—and you're ready for it.**

You can scale confidently.
You can take a real vacation.
You can finally think about succession, sale, or stepping back—not with dread, but with a sense of readiness.

Whatever your version of success looks like, this kind of structure gives you choices.
You don't have to guess. You don't have to hover. You don't have to sacrifice everything else to keep the business going.

Profit stops feeling unpredictable.
Time stops slipping through your fingers.
And you start to feel like the CEO again—not the safety net.

When systems, finances, and people all work together, everything changes.

You stop growing broke. You start growing strong.

The Cost of Waiting

Let's not tiptoe around it—the longer you delay, the more you put at risk.

You've done the work to get clear. You know where the cracks are. You've identified the places where money is leaking, time is being wasted, and responsibilities are getting blurred. You know what needs to change.

But if you stop here—if you close this book and go back to business as usual—that clarity fades fast. And the problems you've uncovered? They don't resolve themselves. They quietly compound.

You can keep hoping that something will shift—that the next big project will create breathing room. That your team will finally "get it." That cash flow will just work itself out.

But hope is not a strategy. And the most successful businesses aren't the ones that hustle the hardest—they're the ones that fix what's broken before it breaks them.

The data backs it up:

- 50% of small businesses fail within five years
- 65% fail within ten

- And 82% of those failures are due to cash flow issues, not lack of effort or passion

> *Most business owners don't fail because they didn't care.*
> *They fail because they waited too long to make a change.*

And the longer you wait, the fewer options you have.
Small inefficiencies turn into major time drains.
Team issues turn into turnover.
Missed metrics become missed paychecks.

Eventually, what was manageable becomes a mess.

But it doesn't have to go that way.

You already have what most CEOs never slow down long enough to find—a clear-eyed view of what's not working and a practical roadmap for what to do about it.

The only question is: **What will you do next?**

Where You Go From Here

Here is your moment to move from clarity into momentum. Not with a massive overhaul. Not with a perfect plan. Just with one decision to keep going.

Choose one area to strengthen.
One small system to improve.

One next move that creates breathing room or builds trust, or improves cash flow.

Because what holds your business together tomorrow isn't more hustle—it's better structure. And the best time to start building it is now.

> *You've come too far to stall here.*
> *Now it's time to take the next step.*

Take that next step—and start building the kind of business that supports your life, protects your time, and gives you back the freedom you've been working so hard to earn.

The freedom to spend your evenings with your family, not your laptop.

The confidence to step away and know things won't fall apart.

The clarity to grow your profits without growing your stress. And the control to decide what's next—whether that's scaling, selling, or simply taking a real vacation without checking in.

When systems support your people, your finances work for you—not against you—and when you're no longer carrying the business alone, everything shifts.

You're no longer growing broke. You're growing strong—on purpose, with clarity, and on your terms.

Turn the page for your next step.

You've got this—and I can't wait to see you finally lead the business you always knew was possible.

Whether you're ready to implement what you've learned, explore deeper support, or revisit the tools that got you here, the next page shows you where to begin.

WHERE TO GO FROM HERE

"The secret of getting ahead is getting started."
— Mark Twain

If something clicked for you in these pages—if you saw your business more clearly, or realized you're not alone in the chaos—then let's keep going.

Every business is different—and so is every next step. Whether you're ready to take action now or want to keep learning at your own pace, here are a few ways we can stay connected.

Let's Stay Connected on LinkedIn Find practical insights, weekly strategy tips, and honest conversations about building a business that works.

linkedin.com/in/karenhairston

Sign Up for My Best Tools by Email

Get short, actionable strategies, real stories from the field, and early access to new programs and resources—sent straight to your inbox.

StopGrowingBroke.net

Grab Free Tools and Resources Online

Visit the site for downloads, quick wins, and deeper dives to help you fix the systems behind your stress and stop growing broke.

https:/resources.StopGrowingBroke.com

Book Your Free Strategy Session

Still testing out the waters? Book a free strategy session today. We'll uncover hidden cash in your business and see if we're a good fit. Even if we're not, you'll walk away with valuable insights you can apply immediately to stop growing broke.

Book your appointment @ StopGrowingBroke.biz.

Explore Deeper Support for Implementation

Ready to stop growing broke and start growing strong on purpose, with clarity, and on your terms? Ready to partner with an expert systems and cash flow consultant?

⭐ Book your appointment @ StopGrowingBroke.biz.

www.ingramcontent.com/pod-product-compliance
Lightning Source LLC
Chambersburg PA
CBHW050506210326
41521CB00011B/2341